C000139934

OWNIN

Owning
God's Word

MARGARET HILLYER

Tollesbury

Book design and production for the publisher by
Bookprint Creative Services, P.O. Box 827, BN21 3YJ, England.
Printed in Great Britain.

Contents

Acknowledgements

The preparation of *Owning God's Word* for publication has enjoyed the attention and energies of many of Margaret's friends. All of these are, one way or another, supporters of Fellowship Afloat, the waterside community to which she gave – and from which received – so much inspiration.

Thanks are due, in particular, to Pat Alexander who edited the text and provided invaluable professional advice; and to others who offered regular encouragement and expertise. In recent months, I have been grateful to many good friends and family who nudged me on through the last stages of preparation. And I am confident that I can say all this on behalf of Margaret, who herself received great encouragement and confidence from those who enjoyed her "scribblings", as she called them.

The profits from the sale of *Owning God's Word* will go to Fellowship Afloat Charitable Trust, to further the Christian ministry onboard the former lightvessel *Trinity*.

David Hillyer

About Margaret and this Book

Margaret was born on 28 July 1946, into a Gloucestershire farm worker's family. In her own words:

I was brought up in the Cotswolds, deep in the country, where I lived with my parents, my brother, and an uncle and grandfather. My mother took me to Sunday School in the village Methodist Chapel, two miles away whenever she could, and I was christened there when I was four. There, and in the local village school, I grew up hearing Bible stories every day. My mother gave me a great love of reading, and a love for Bible stories which I always believed to be true.

My father was a farm worker and it was a struggle for my parents to send me to the grammar school, keep me on through the sixth form and support my going to college – not just financially, but culturally. My mother was considered to be "snooty", encouraging my education.

I went to Teacher Training College in Lincolnshire, far enough from home to make coming home difficult – not because I didn't want to come home, but because I feared that I would be homesick and want to come home every weekend. On my first night I came back to my room to find my new room mate sitting up in bed reading her Bible. I was a bit surprised by this and asked her why. We talked far into the night, as she basically told me that to be a Christian I needed to ask forgiveness for my sins, ask Jesus into my life.

Through my teens I had begun to feel that there was a bit more to church than listening to boring sermons and prayers, but had been unable to discover what it was. I couldn't understand how I had never realised what Jesus being a Saviour meant.

If at that point God had written my name in the sky as proof that he had 'come into my life' it might have been easier. I just couldn't seem to believe that Jesus would do that for me. So when I needed a bit of faith I relied on my friend's, and the rest of the time I was frightened that, if Jesus really did come into my life, I might have to give a few things up.

I went to the local Baptist Church with other Christians and became quite involved in their circle, but standing a little on the outside. After about 14 months, I gave up the unequal struggle and agreed that if I had asked Jesus into my life, then he must have come in! It was good, I belonged. But I was a long way from really knowing Jesus.

I then moved up to Norfolk to start teaching in a small village school, and went to the local Baptist Church. There I began to grow a little in my faith, as I got to know folk in the church, and one family in particular encouraged and challenged me.

Margaret's next post was at Harestreet County Primary School in Harlow, where she became involved with Oakwood Chapel. It was at Oakwood that she met David, who was about to start a three-year teacher-training course. In the years that followed Margaret became an enthusiastic part of the Christian ministry at the church and was a friend to many.

She married David in 1975, setting up home in Tollesbury where David was the Warden of Fellowship Afloat Charitable Trust – which runs residential dinghy sailing and outdoor activity courses for schools and youth clubs. Margaret taught in Tollesbury County Primary School, gradually becoming more and more absorbed into the work of Fellowship Afloat.

In 1979 Margaret left teaching to run the galley and office

for Fellowship Afloat, serving a busy apprenticeship with the face-to-face residential work onboard *Memory*, the Trust's accommodation base. Her responsibilities later focused on the administration and book keeping for the Trust. Margaret and David were blessed to work together, as a team, complementing one another in so many ways.

> Our mission was very much to share faith and this was done to a great extent by sharing activities with young people, and trying to relate our faith to every day life. "Thought for the Day", chatting about faith in a dinghy, the galley, the saloon, walking up the path, enjoying God's creation – exhausted, seeing each other at our worst – all part of making our faith relevant to everyday life. For me it was a time of giving out, and I now realise how important the teaching that I had received as a young Christian had been. It enabled me to survive, and it made me aware of the power of the prayers of those who supported our work.

In 1985 Margaret wrote *Salt in the Air*, a book that told the story of Fellowship Afloat – it celebrated and publicised the work of the Trust and remains a very precious record of how God led the waterside community though its formative years.

Margaret enjoyed many local church and community responsibilities: playing the church organ, participating in the work of the Lighthouse Christian Bookshop, speaking at women's meetings – and she was also a local school governor for a short time.

Deep friendships made through Fellowship Afloat and in the local community were a hallmark of Margaret's life. All who knew her will miss her warm and welcoming smile – and her practical, down-to-earth outlook on life. She firmly believed that there is a "God-shaped space" in everyone – a basic longing which she took every opportunity to encourage and nurture.

Her love of the scriptures led Margaret into biblical studies, which then developed into writing personal reflections on Bible passages. This work deepened her own faith, especially as she shared her discoveries with other people.

I had been reading the Bible through each year for several years, as well as trying to read it more meditatively.

At the heart of Fellowship Afloat is the desire to share the good news of Jesus with our visitors, who are mainly young people. Our faith needs to be relevant and it needs to be for every day, not just Sundays. Earning the right to share our faith is important. Spending time with people, building relationships, enjoying activities with each other, looking after each other, being interested in each other, valuing and respecting each other, are all part of living our faith.

I've come to realise that fewer people read the Bible, particularly young people, and you often hear the question: "How is the Bible relevant now?" One of the things I have been able to do is to let the Bible "come at me" in a way that makes it relevant to my life. It speaks to me about where I am. I want other people to capture that reality.

Because the Bible has been important to me – in fact during a particularly dark period in my life it seemed to be all of God that I had to hang on to – I long for it to be important to other people. There may be lots of different ways of reading it, but if we allow the Holy Spirit to open the Bible up to us, I think it *reads us* rather than the other way round. More than anything I want to be able share the Bible and my experience of what faith in a personal God means in a way that makes it real to people and leads them to experience the great love that God has for each one of us.

Margaret put her finishing touches to this book just three days before she died, peacefully at home on 5 February 2004, with David beside her.

On 13 February 2004 more than 400 friends and family

gathered at Tollesbury Congregational Church to celebrate and give thanks for Margaret's life. The occasion was made all the more poignant by the many friends who read the reflections on Bible passages which Margaret had written.

Pat Alexander

PART ONE

Owning the Psalms

1

God's message comes to me in new words

One day I suddenly found that a passage from God's word "came at me" in the most amazing way – in completely different words, and in a way which mirrored exactly how I was feeling.

I was reading a small section from Psalm 119 (verses 25–32) over and over again because I was so fascinated by the first line: "My soul clings to the dust". My soul was certainly clinging to the dust. In fact I felt that it was getting *buried* in the dust. I thought: "That's it, Lord. I'm flat on my face!"

Then I began to read the rest of the verses again, changing them into different words in my head as I realised that I had come to God's word for help, doubting that I would find it. I was completely mesmerised and very excited – I grabbed a pen and started to write down the words because I was frightened I would forget them. This was the result:

Psalm 119:25–32 "I'm flat on my face, Lord!"

I'm flat on my face, Lord; can your word pick me up?
I've said how wilful I am; amazingly, you are still willing to
  talk to me.
Open your word to me and make it live.
Open my eyes to the truth.
Hide these things deep within my heart so that I can mull
  them over.

I am so sad, so bowed down with all my trouble.
Your word says I needn't be, so how does this happen?

Don't let me keep kidding myself.
Help me to be honest about myself to others.
People think I am what I'm not.
I like to hide behind that, and yet I hate it: I want to
    be me.
I want people to see me as I am.
Help me to reveal the real me.
A long time ago now, Lord, I decided to follow you.
I decided that you were who you said you were.
I wanted you to have my life.
I have tried to see life as you would; I've often failed.
I have tried to read your word – all of it, even when it
    didn't make sense.
Where are you, Lord?
Have I really got it wrong?
I will still try to do what you want me to do.
Make my heart big enough to cope,
Especially when what you want me to do seems too hard.

This was amazing. It was exactly how I felt. It was my life story.
It was where I was at. This bit of Psalm 119 was for me – I
owned it. God understood that I was discouraged and fed up
and, if he understood, he would help me. He was telling me
that the psalmist, living all those hundreds of years ago, had
felt just like me.

Like me, the psalmist had made a decision to follow God.
He had struggled to study God's word, and yet had begun to
wonder if it all made sense after all. So God understood exactly
how I was feeling.

It had taken me rather a long time to get to this point. I had been a Christian for many years. I had listened to a lot of preachers and I had read a lot of books. I had a theology which I felt comfortable with and a God I trusted, though often in a fairly casual way. In so many ways my faith in God had become my bedrock. Yet I still seemed to have some hang-ups about reading the Bible. I never seemed to have any insight into the Bible myself; I was always dependent on what others said. Even though I believed the Bible was God's word and that it was important for me to read it, I easily found excuses not to. In any case, what I read didn't really impact on my life. I was questioning myself and God, and wondering if I was believing in a fairy story. Of course this is a feeling that we all have from time to time. We don't like to admit it to anyone, least of all God – but here he was telling me that it was OK. He knew how I felt, and I was not alone. It was a new beginning.

Now I had read a passage that had made a huge impact on me. It was absolutely relevant to what was happening in my life and I was very excited. Then I began to feel a bit scared.

What had happened?

Had God spoken to me? Had he really given me those words? Where did they come from? It was a bit presumptuous to think that God's Holy Spirit had given me the words. I wasn't anyone special; I wasn't a spiritual giant; I hadn't spent hours in prayer seeking God's special blessing. Yet, instead of *me reading* the Bible, I felt that *it was reading me*. I knew exactly how the psalmist felt – it could have been me writing. In fact, this short passage was my life story on a page and I had just written it.

2

Can it happen again?

I didn't tell anyone what had happened. It was probably just one of those things; just the way I was feeling at the time. But the more I thought about it and tried to talk to God about it, the more convinced I became that he had given me something very special, a word *just for me*. I felt that I had been blessed in a very special way. It was my little secret with God.

A few days later, just as I was beginning to forget my excitement and feel that maybe God had just wanted to encourage me, I found myself reading Proverbs 3. The first verse says: "My son, do not forget my law, but let your heart keep my commands." Straightaway the first line jumped out at me as: *"Don't forget to listen to God and respond to him."* "Here we go again," I thought, and got out my pen.

Proverbs 3:1–18 Trust is the bottom line

> Don't forget to listen to God and respond to him.
> Then you will achieve what you want; you will
>   have peace.
> Be true to yourself, put others first,
> And don't be distracted from doing what is right.
> Open your heart to what Jesus wants of you,
> And God will honour you, and so will other people.
> Know that God will never, ever let you down,

However difficult, strange, and hard to understand life is.
Even when everything appears to be going wrong!
Even if nothing happens when you think it should!
Even if you think it is now or never and God doesn't seem
    to be doing anything!
Even if things seem totally impossible!
God has got everything under control
And you'd better believe it!
Make sure you own up to thinking that God is important
    in your life.
Don't be afraid to talk about him.
Don't be ashamed, or awkward
About thinking he's the greatest.
Everything will be OK; the pieces of the jigsaw will fit.

That was pretty powerful and, for me, a very clear message that
I wasn't to keep all this to myself. Somehow I had to share it.
The context of my reading was trust and the title I had written
down was "Trust is the bottom line." So I had to trust God that
this was for real.

I was a bit puzzled how to share. Did it mean that I would
do some more of this "writing in my own words"? I soon
discovered that the answer to this was "yes" and, after a while,
when I had done about a dozen pieces of writing, I thought
maybe it was time to obey that instruction to share.

I am in a very privileged position working for a Christian
organisation where we meet at the beginning of the day,
someone gives a thought, and we talk and pray about the day's
activities and anything else that seems important. Very soon it
was my turn to give a "thought". So I plucked up my courage,
and decided to use the first piece that I wrote from Psalm 119.
I felt that it would help me to share some of my struggles and
encourage others in theirs. I could only explain my rendering

of these verses from the psalm by talking about God understanding how we felt, understanding how the psalmist felt,
and how these words had helped and encouraged me to realise
that God understood how I felt too. As I had read it in the New
King James Version originally, I read that first, and then read
what I had written.

If you are going to try something out, it is always good to be
among friends when you do it, and it is fantastic to be encouraged. Although I was unable to explain properly what I had
written, or how, it was so good to share. Everyone was very
appreciative. They suggested that it was a bit like a paraphrase.
I knew that these were not paraphrases, because I had not
delved into the original meaning of the passage or studied the
background or the original language. However, it was good to
know that hearing the passage in these different words was
helpful to other people too. I began to feel more confident
about "my scribblings".

3

New confidence and a surer faith

When I first became a Christian I worried a lot about reading the Bible. People seemed to be saying that I should now be able to understand the Bible in a new way. God would speak to me through it and I would find guidance in it for the things that puzzled me. The Holy Spirit would reveal his word to me. I would be able to read a passage, and some deep and meaningful thought would come to me.

At this point, as a very new and frightened Christian, I went to a big student Christian conference where I was assigned to a Bible Study group. We read a passage about the Good Shepherd. Then the leader started to ask us questions and I was petrified she would ask me and I wouldn't know the answer. She did ask me and I didn't know the answer, but someone else did and it was so easy and straightforward! I felt absolutely dreadful. How could I possibly be a Christian? If I really were a Christian, wouldn't the Holy Spirit have given me the answer?

The scars of that experience were still with me when I began what, to me, was a very exciting understanding of what some passages of the Bible said to me. I so often felt that perhaps I was not a "proper Christian". I didn't find it very easy to pray out loud in a group, although my faith had obviously grown over the years, and I had learnt a lot about the Bible from inspiring preachers and from good and wise friends. Yet I never felt able to learn things from the Bible by myself. I had decided that I was just someone who liked to sit at people's feet and learn. But that was not actually true: I'm really a person who likes to discover things for herself.

This amazing new way of reading the Bible was very precious to me. It was as if God was giving me a very special blessing and encouraging me by saying, "You can do it" – much as we might encourage a small child to have a go at something they found challenging. I seemed to be setting out on a journey of self-discovery, learning things about myself that I had not realised.

One of my favourite psalms is Psalm 37, and a verse I have often pondered over is verse 4: "Delight in the Lord and he will give you the desires of your heart." Well, he was certainly giving me the desires of my heart. But this psalm isn't just about us getting what we want – it means business – there are some hard lessons in it.

As I found myself writing the familiar verses in new words, I discovered that I am very critical of other Christians and how they live their lives. I can be so judgemental of others, thinking that I am so much better than they are. This psalm is quite straightforward about how God views this. I was put firmly in my place and my thinking was completely turned around. I need to remind myself often of what this psalm said to me.

Psalm 37:1–4 Mind your own business and God will mind *you*

> Don't spend time judging other people *you* think have
> got it all wrong,
> Who *you* think are disobeying God.
> Don't get uptight about people who do evil and
> wicked things.
> They won't last for ever and they will not prosper.

If you are going to occupy your mind at all with them,
You should feel sorry for them!
Take Jesus as your example,
Believe he is who he says he is, and follow him.
Do what he says.
Live life to the full.
Live in the place where you are,
And joyfully, purposefully proclaim his name.
Never doubt that God is with you.
He will never let you down.
He will honour you.
He will keep you.
He will bless you.
Take delight in all that is yours:
Your way of life, your job, your possessions –
Because he has given them to you.
But most of all – enjoy his presence.
Acknowledge that he is with you, in you,
And enjoy the company.
Share what you're doing
And he will give you life abundant – every good thing,
Joy beyond measure, everything you want.
He will fulfil your deepest longings.

We can be critical of others in so many ways. We can feel
superior or inferior – neither way is right.

If, like me, you need some assurance that you can do things,
that what you are doing is important to God, that he is involved
in the nitty gritty of everyday life, these first four verses from
Psalm 37 are so encouraging, so affirming. How easy it is to
look at other people and think they have got it all together and
you haven't; or the other way round. Maybe this psalm is really
David (the psalmist) trying to encourage himself that all those

evil people around him will not prevail, that he just needs to trust in the Lord for himself. But it was certainly making me see that I looked at other Christians, never mind the world in general, and made judgements. I really didn't need to do that. I don't need to compare myself with other people, or feel inferior. I need to look at God. And he says I'm OK.

Psalm 37:5–11 If it's OK with God, it's OK!

Make sure you consult God about what you do.
Make sure he approves, make sure you're doing it
    for him.
Believe that he is interested, that he is involved,
That he cares about what you are doing.
And he will make sure it goes OK.
He will sort it out.

And if people question your motives, if they criticise you,
As long as you know it's OK with God, it's OK.
One day he'll reveal the truth to others.
Meanwhile you will be righteous – right in Christ,
And the fact will shine forth as a blinding light.
It will be abundantly clear.
Nothing will be hidden as it would be in the darkness
    of night.
It will be bright as the middle of the day,
And justice will be seen by all.
You will be seen as just.

So settle down with God and relax.
Wait for him to sort it out.
Don't get all upset, wanting to speak up for yourself,
Explaining everything,

Trying to make people understand where you're
　　coming from.
Don't worry if other people are more popular,
Seem to get on better, have a good time,
Especially if they are listening to others and not to God.
Righteous indignation is not for you.
If you feel wronged or misunderstood – never mind.
Don't be cross about it.
God knows what's in your heart –
Don't get involved –
TRUST GOD for everything.
It's *his* approval you need, not anyone else's.

We are God's heirs – his inheritance is for us.
His inheritance is the whole earth.
Everything that is his is ours.
Evil people who deny that God exists –
They won't inherit it.

These words were a great confirmation to me that God was at
work in my life. I did not have to worry what other people
were thinking and feel inferior. God knew what was deep in my
heart and, even if it was not quite what he wanted, we could
work on it together.

Gradually all those hang-ups that I had about not being a
real Christian, about not being able to understand God's word,
began to fade, and I began to realise that here was God,
showing me his word in a new way, so that it was for me.

Yes, it was *David's psalm*, it was about his situation, and it
goes on to speak much more about the good and the bad. But
these first eleven verses were what God wanted to say to me,
and now I had them in words which were for me – it was
almost like finding my words behind David's words.

4

Spending time with God's word – just "hanging in"

We all read our Bibles in different ways and for different reasons. An important turning-point for me was when I read about someone who had started reading the Bible through once, sometimes twice, in a year.

"Just think," he said, "if you start when you are 20, by the time you are 40 you will have read it through 20 times." Well, I was 40-something already and had quite a bit of catching up to do! But I was challenged to start. In fact I was so challenged by the fact that I had probably lived at least half of my life and had never read the Bible through once, that I read it in six months.

I read it in Kenneth Taylor's paraphrase, *The Living Bible*, because I figured that if I had to read it through as a story, it might be a good idea to make it as easy as possible to understand. This meant that I had to read about five chapters a day, and I noticed that there are more words in *The Living Bible* than in the formal translations. So it was hard going, and sometimes I hadn't a clue what I'd read, particularly in Leviticus – all those rules and regulations – or when I reached Chronicles and found myself thinking "haven't I read this somewhere before?" Each day I read my allotted bit and sometimes it went in my eyes and straight out of my head. But for me it was a turning-point.

I then resolved to read it in a year and used my New King James Version.

Then I went on to read it chronologically with a bit of help from Selwyn Hughes.[1] This was when I realised why I kept thinking things were repeated in the Old Testament. They are – sometimes several times. Each year I would read the Bible through, in a slightly different way each time, and each year I seemed to read things I'd never read before.

I suppose it was all a bit frenetic really. I often read out of a sense of guilt and duty, often in a hurry, but despite this God was very patient and, when he saw his chance, got involved in my reading in a way that I never expected, or thought was possible. I'm so glad, because after a few years of all this hectic reading, although I was getting the big picture, an overview of the whole Bible, I wasn't really reading it in a way that had an impact on my life.

So I started to slow down a bit. Despite the fact that I had vowed I'd never use a daily reading scheme again – I'd always spent more time reading the notes than reading the Bible – I started to use *Every Day With Jesus*,[2] notes I was familiar with and found helpful. Most Bible reading notes seem to follow a similar format: a catchy title, a short text from a passage, then the writer's thoughts about the passage, a prayer and then a few extra passages to read if you want to. I felt this might give a bit more structure and guidance to my reading. I confess that, if I was in a hurry, I would just read the text, and then Selwyn Hughes' thought. It didn't take me long to fall into my old trap.

However, I had begun to feel that I must make more effort to spend time, so I started to write notes, not only from the Bible Notes but some of my own thoughts from the passage. Gradually I began to read everything twice.

It was because I had read that passage from Psalm 119 several times that it came at me so differently. Somehow this experience showed me that I am precious to God and he wants to be my friend. It was great to have this lovely assurance from God. It made me realise that during all those long hours of reading, God had been able to bless. It seemed such a long time before God did this, but it was worth it.

Here's another psalm – Psalm 40 – that just about sums this up. As it "came at me" in different words, it made me understand this idea a little more.

Psalm 40 Waiting for God

It was such a long time before God answered me.
I seemed to have to cry out for ever,
But what else could I do?
It was as if I had sunk into a quicksand,
And the harder I struggled the deeper I went.
I was just hanging in there.
But when he finally answered,
He certainly sorted things out in a very spectacular way.
I didn't really think it was possible.
Suddenly I had a new direction and I was safe.
Now I keep singing and shouting how wonderful God is.
Most people think I've gone crazy; they're a bit scared
    of me.
But some recognize the amazing miracle that God has
    done for me.
And so they want to throw in their lot with God too.
They realise that he can help them.
How wonderful it is for the person who steps
    towards God
And takes no notice of what people say about them –
That they are crazy to believe in God.
And then I find myself lost for words.
You are so amazing, Lord.

You are involved in our everyday lives.
We are in your thoughts –
You care about what is happening to each one of us.
How do you *do* that?
I used to think you were fierce and demanding
And that you would punish me if I didn't do the
    right thing –
Whatever that was.
But you are not like that.
You love me.
You have written my name in your special book
And no-one can rub it out.
Your way is for me, Lord.
Your work is for me too, to help and encourage me.
So I have some amazing news to tell:
This special offer is not just for me;
It's for everyone.
So what is my great message?
You never let me down,
I am yours for ever
And you love me.
I can't bear to think what it would be like if you didn't.
I need your love, and the truth of your love, to keep
    me safe.
Otherwise I can't cope.
Everything is too much and it overwhelms me.
I can't do anything without you.
So it's over to you, Lord, as usual
And please don't be too long.
Those things which threaten me
And those people who challenge me –
They are your problem, Lord.
That's the way you want it to be.

As for those of us who love you, Lord,
Who acknowledge all you have done for us,
Help us to thank you properly, Lord.
I can never forget that you love me, Lord,
That I can't manage on my own
And amazingly you make *my* business *your* business.
You are always ready and able to help.
I just need to learn patience and trust,
For you will never let me down.

[1] Selwyn Hughes, *Through the Bible in a Year*, CWR
[2] Selwyn Hughes, *Every Day with Jesus – Daily Bible Reading Notes*, CWR

5

When I'm tired and feeling down

You might think that now everything would be easy, and that life would be one long encouragement. Sadly this has not been so – after all, we are human, and this means that we don't live in perfection. Life can still be hard. We can still lose our way a bit. One day, when I was feeling very weary and discouraged, I read this verse:

> *"For consider him who endured such hostility from sinners against himself, lest you become weary and discouraged in your souls"* (Hebrews 12:3).

That was it – I had become weary and discouraged in my soul. At first, I was surprised to find this verse here. Surely Jesus had never felt weary and discouraged. Then I remembered – Jesus was fully human, and he endured a great deal more in every way than I ever will. I had not suffered as Jesus had, nor fought the kind of battle he had. I had not struggled against sin to the point where it cost me my life (Hebrews 12:4). But I was so weary – weary in my body, weary in my emotions, weary in my innermost being, weary in my soul – and I wanted to give up.

I had been feeling that way for quite a while, so to find the phrase in this verse startled me out of my despondency – I wondered if I knew what *weary* really meant. I needed the Lord

to restore my soul, that was for sure. Then I found Psalm 30
reflecting these feelings back at me.

Psalm 30 God is who he says he is

I know that you are God
And I will say so.
For you always pick me up when I fall down.
And you make me better.
How I cry out to you!
"Oh Lord!"
And then I don't know what else to say.
"Oh Lord!"
And you make it all right.
Somehow I survive.
I don't quite go over the edge,
Somehow you hang on to me.
We are your saints
And we really should praise you.
We really should be thankful –
Thankful that you bothered with us,
Thankful that you have given your most holy name to us.
Wow!
You must get so fed up with us;
Probably angry as well.
But only for a moment.
It doesn't last –
It can't,
Because you love us so much.
After all, you have chosen us,
You have given us your most holy name
And it is for ever.
You won't take it back.

We may be sad and weep,
And you will weep too,
But it will not last.
Joy will follow, eventually.
You see, Lord –
When everything's OK I'm quite sure of myself,
You bless me enormously,
And then I am strong.
But when you hide your face awhile –
Crash –
Am I in trouble?
And then I cry out to you;
I question you.
How can you let me fall?
How can you abandon me?
Where are you?
Why is this happening to me?
So many questions – I'm sorry.
But you see –
I want you to be real, Lord.
I want to know you are there.
I want to know that my sorrow will be turned to joy.
I should not be moaning, should I?
And down in the mouth!
Make me glad, Lord,
For I want my very being to sing,
To sing your praise,
To shout that you are God.
That you are who you say you are.

6

The "wow" factor

I found it all too easy, now, to feel very pleased with myself. Wasn't God giving me very special insight into his word? I must be getting to know him better. He must be pleased with me. Oh dear! The reality is, of course, that God was helping me to understand more about his word and himself: it was all of God and none of me. Why do we always want to make ourselves important?

We like to think we have all the answers, too – that we know it all. It is easy to come to the Bible like this. We ask the questions, but we have already decided the answers. We approach things in a logical way – we ask our questions about who God is – and we get the answers we expect. It was because I had found myself waiting on God a bit more, instead of rushing off in my own direction, that I had started to read the Bible so differently.

God is a very personal God. He wants to surprise us. He wants to treat us individually. He wants us to be open to him. He wants us to say "Wow!"

It is as I have tried to be open to God and his word that I have discovered things I never imagined. I have discovered that God's word *reads me*, rather than *me reading it*. I have discovered that he is able to reflect back a word of comfort, encouragement, understanding, identification, that seems to be for me alone. The same verse or passage may say something else to you, because God's word is living, not dead, and it will be relevant to you and your situation.

Some people may describe this reflection of mine as meditation, but that makes it sound like hard work and a very holy occupation. In a way it is, but if we allow ourselves to unpack the word "meditation" and consider it in its simplicity, in words we can relate to more easily, it will help us to see that there isn't really any great mystery about it. To meditate is to reflect on things, to ponder things, giving time for thoughts to develop. If we read the Bible and allow ourselves time to think about what we've read, not just at a superficial level, but asking questions and waiting for some possible answers to come to us, then we begin to allow God to speak to us.

I think I am most surprised when I read a familiar passage, and suddenly I find it saying something different. I think I already know what it is saying and I am not looking for anything else, and then – "Pow!" – it says a little extra. Something I had not expected. And then I say "Wow"!

Psalm 42 was like that. It is so familiar – we even sing a hymn that is based on the beginning almost word for word. And if I'm truthful I have often found myself slightly embarrassed to be singing the words. Do I really mean them? Am I really "panting for God"? I started to think what it must be like to be a thirsty deer, what it would be like to be thirsty, really thirsty, myself. By the time I had finished writing I was completely gobsmacked.

Psalm 42 God is thirsty *for me*!

I am so thirsty.
I need a drink.
How much longer before I can have some water?
How much longer can I last?

My mouth is so dry;
I feel so weak;
I *must* have a drink.

Just imagine a long cool drink of ice-cold refreshing
    fruit juice.
Lovely clear water with bubbles popping to the surface,
The fizz splashing your face.
The feel of fresh, tasty water
Bubbling on your tongue.

This is how thirsty I am for you, Lord.
I know what it will be like
When you answer at last.
That's what keeps me going when everyone taunts me.
No-one believes in you, Lord.
They think I am putting my trust in a fairy tale.
But I know that you are a person, Lord.
I have known what it was like to be with others who loved
    and worshiped you.
But now I'm on my own.
And it's such a struggle all by myself.
No-one to encourage me.
I know that I should not be so discouraged,
But it's hard, Lord,
Especially when I don't seem to feel you very near.
Where are you, Lord?
Why don't you come and talk to me?
I know that you will – in the end.

I just have to remember the things you have done
    in the past:
The power of your creation,

The mountains, the waterfalls, the ocean,
The greatness of such things
Reflecting the depth of your very great love.
I can know your lovingkindness
As I live each day.
I can hear your quiet song at night as I fall asleep.
You are there when I pray.

I know that you are listening,
So why don't you answer?
Why do you not remove my enemies from me?
The enemies of doubt and fear;
The enemies of temptation and depression.

You *want* me to be thirsty, don't you, Lord?
You *want* me to trust you.
You want *me*!
You want to save me from myself.
You want to save me for yourself.

Suddenly I realised that *God was thirsty for me* – wow! – he just
needed me to return the compliment a bit more, instead of
feeling sorry for myself because life was difficult.

7

"Honestly, God . . ."

Just as I have found it difficult to acknowledge that I have a thirst for God, so I have found the word *sin* difficult to use all by itself. It is very easy to find substitute words. In some ways that can be a healthy thing, but we have to come back to the word sin in the end.

In his Sermon on the Mount Jesus says, "Blessed are the pure in heart, for they will see God" (Matthew 5:8). J. B. Phillips translates this as being utterly sincere. Being sincere makes me think about the motives that I might have for doing things; what I really think about things; being honest with God. There's no point in being anything other than honest with God, and yet so often we try to hide things from him.

Two psalms have helped me with these thoughts. The first is Psalm 32. As I owned the words of this psalm, I was able to tell God for the first time how bad I really felt, realising that I was not alone – someone else had felt the same way.

Psalm 32 God can make it all right

What a relief!
I've done something really dreadful,
And I can't undo it.
I've said something awful and hurtful,
And the more I try to put it right

The worse it is.
I feel really bad.
My heart sinks –
A wave of dreadfulness sweeps through my whole being.
And then God takes over.

I really didn't mean to upset –
I just put both feet in it before I could stop myself.
Now I don't know what to do;
I feel worse and worse.
The whole thing weighs on my mind.
It occupies every waking thought –
It won't go away.
I feel bleak and helpless.
And then I realise that God understands.

He can mend things;
He can stand in the gap.
If I just spill it all out to him,
Let him take over,
He will be there for me.
He will comfort.
He will heal.
He will help.
And how he longs for me to listen to him –
To stop rushing into life
Thinking I have all the answers,
Thinking I know best.
Consider the Lord,
Consider *his* ways.
Consider what he would do.
And then, maybe
I won't make such big mistakes,

Won't get it wrong quite so often.
God will be able to keep me out of trouble.
And then,
Instead of that sinking feeling I get so often
When I realise I've messed it up once more,
I can be full of joy!
I can hold my head up high.
I can be happy and content.

Like so many psalms, this one starts off with a sense of desperation – then the writer realises that God is who he says he is and is able to help, to come up trumps, to provide a solution.

We come to realise a little of the graciousness of God, the sheer lovingkindness he has towards us. It's a great word – "lovingkindness"– I just love it.

I often find myself taking down addresses on the telephone, or giving my own. Sometimes it's something like "Cherrydown" – all one word. That made me think about "lovingkindness" – all one word – and how much is wrapped up in that word. I then read Psalm 51 in a new light. The words became a kind of healing balm for my soul.

Psalm 51:1–17 "Spring-cleaned" with lovingkindness

"Lovingkindness" – all one word.
That is what you treat me with,
That is how you cope with me.
I am smothered with bad things –
Bad thoughts,
Bad feelings,
Bad actions,
Bad words –
And you blot them all up

With your endless tenderness,
Love,
And kindness.

I am only too well aware
Of all the badness in my life.
I am reminded so often
Of the things I've done wrong,
Of the people I've hurt.
And it is you I have hurt most of all,
Wilfully turning away from you,
Doing what *I* want to do –
Sometimes kidding myself
It is what you want me to do.
You are right
When you show me that I am wrong.
I deserve you to punish me.
Was I born full of self –
Wanting my own way –
From the beginning?
You want me to be otherwise.
You long to fill me with knowledge
And love of you.
You long that I should desire to follow truth,
To long for you in my inmost being.

Well, Lord,
You need to sort me out.
I need a spring-clean
In every part.
And if you do that,
Then I *will* be clean,
Even though I am so filthy.

Can I ever be clean?
I have been so deaf to your voice,
I have been so crippled by my own wilful ways.
Can you wash me clean?
Can you still see my sin?
Can you really wipe it all away?
You can!

Start me off afresh, Lord,
With a sparkling clean heart.
Renew my determination to follow you.
Strengthen it.
Set it in the steel of your love.
Please let me be with you;
Please don't go away.
Please give me back your joy.
Your joy.
I didn't look after it very well,
And you removed it;
But in your generosity,
And lovingkindness,
You return
And hold me tight.
Lord, I will tell everyone about you.
I will tell everyone what you have done for me
How great you are!
And they will want to know you
For themselves.
Don't let me dwell in the past and be ashamed.
For you have saved me from all that,
And I *must* move on.
I will give praise and honour to you by talking about you.
For that is what you require of me;

Not that I try to get myself clean,
For I continually grovel around in my filth,
And becoming clean is impossible.
You just want me to be really sorry,
To turn right round and start afresh.
And in your lovingkindness,
You will start over again with me.

As I acknowledged my need for a spring-clean, it was very liberating, It was really releasing to consider my sin against God's lovingkindness. I realised once again how important I was to God, as I thought about the lengths he has gone to to deal with the sin, yes sin, that I find attached to myself.

8

Reading with expectation and excitement

I don't "rewrite" every passage of the Bible that I read, but I do come to the Bible with an expectation that it will understand me. I come expecting it to say something to me. I come expecting to meet with God.

Sometimes it is when I most need something special from God that a passage will leap out at me. Other times I think I simply need to be expectant. Often I feel let down or discouraged by life around me, distracted by the busyness of life and frustrated that I don't spend more time with God. I don't read the Bible as much as I could, and I often feel like giving up. That's because I'm human. Even though God does great things for us, even though we have lots to be thankful for, we don't always feel on top of the world.

I was reading Psalm 143 when the verse which says "my soul thirsts for you like a parched land" jumped out at me, not because it was true, but because I wished it was. And finding the words "O Lord" in the first line made me read the psalm more carefully. I often find myself saying "O Lord" and then get no further – I don't know what else to say.

Psalm 143:1–12 "I give up!"

O Lord.
That's usually all I can manage.
O Lord – please – are you listening?
I know you are listening,
But I need a bit of reassurance.
I know you are faithful to me.
But I am so unfaithful to you –
I can hardly believe it.
I know you are far removed from me,
And yet brought near by the death of your dear Son.
I can't bear to think what you really think of me,
Even though I know I have been made right with you –
Jesus has done that!
Even so, no-one can be righteous alongside you.
And I don't think I can cope
With the person I really am.

Satan has prowled round about
Like a roaring lion
With his no-good message.
I feel I have to get everything right,
Everything sorted,
Before I can ask you to answer.
Not true!
But I want to give up,
Stop struggling.
I feel crushed and ready to give up.
And life seems very dark and dead.
No joy,
No light,
No life.

And I feel overwhelmed with sadness and distress.
My heart is weary,
And I don't know what to do.

Things weren't always like this, were they?
If I read your word
It does speak to me and bring comfort –
But then
The effort to open your word
Seems too much.
I see your handiwork around me;
I often look up at the stars
And wonder –
And I want to spread out my hands,
Thinking that that will give you a way in to my self.
And I'm scared you won't come.
My soul longs for you like a thirsty land,
I know it does.
And yet I doubt
That I really do long for you more than anything else.
Surely I'm not kidding myself
If I say, *"I long for you."*

I need your help, Lord!
Please answer quickly before I give up.
You seem so far away.
Come close and show your face to me.
Otherwise
I'm really scared that I'll give up.
I would love to know your lovingkindness in the morning,
Start my day with love from you.
Often my day starts with a nightmare and distress.
Speak to me in my sleep,

And wake me with peace and contentment.
For you can do this – I know.

Show me what I should really be doing.
It can't be what I'm doing at the moment,
Full of fear and distress.
How do I lift up my soul to you?
How do I come to you for help?
How do I hide in you?
More than anything, I want to do your will,
Walk your way –
Please help me.

Show me,
Teach me.
Your Spirit is good
And does dwell within me.
Please help me to know
And acknowledge this.

I need your revival, Lord.
Renew and revive my love!
Renew and revive my commitment!
Renew and revive my enthusiasm!
Renew and revive my faith!
Renew and revive my energy!

Please get me out of trouble, Lord;
Because you've said you can
And you will –
Because I acknowledge your righteousness,
Because I want to glorify your name,
Because I want to serve you.

It was a particular comfort to me that someone else understood about bad dreams and horrible mornings. When I was pondering this psalm and coming up with a new way of reading it, it was a time in my life when I often felt particularly distressed when I woke up in the morning, and I would recall dreams of frustration and fear. Usually, as the day wore on, I gradually began to feel better and by the evening I would almost have forgotten the feelings of the morning.

This psalm helped me to feel more confident that God was still with me and in control; it helped me to get God's perspective instead of my own on some of the stresses that were encroaching on my life. It didn't happen overnight, but this psalm was the beginning of healing.

Once again it was as if God had spoken to my soul – he understood just how I felt. This was a psalm written thousands of years ago and yet I could make it my prayer today.

9

As good as a hug

Sometimes I need a hug. We all do – but maybe there is no-one to hug us. I think God can always give us a hug, and I have discovered that God's word can actually give me a hug too. This part of Psalm 119 has a great descripion of how the Bible can do that.

Psalm 119:129–136 God's word holds me close

Your word is brilliant.
It is not just there for me to read;
It is as if it is inside me, safe.
It seeps into the very depths of my being –
And stays there.
It's a bit like invisible ink when you put it in the heat.
Suddenly you can see what it says.
I don't need to ask complicated questions –
I just need to read your word.
I long to know what you want me to do,
How you want me to live.
And there it is, all in your word –
I just need to read it.

Why don't I just do that?
How can I let you down and disappoint you?

Please bear with me, for I do love you.

Don't give up on me.
Somehow bring me back to your word.
Show me the instruction I need
So that I know which way to go,
What to do next.
Keep me from going the wrong way
And don't let me give up.
Don't let me do what I know is wrong.
Help me to be strong
And have the courage of my convictions.
Don't let me be swayed by what other people say
    or think.
I need to measure things against your yardstick.

And just sometimes, Lord,
I need to know that you are pleased with me,
I need a hug, a gentle encouragement.

How sad it is – so disappointing, tragic even –
To think what little notice people take of your word.
They ignore it and they miss such a lot.
They miss everything
Because they take no notice
Of the instruction manual that goes with life.

I find myself longing more and more for people to read God's word – to discover its riches, its mysteries, its comforts, its ability to meet us where we are and give us a hug if we need it. There are many who do this, but I suspect that there are plenty who, like me, have to learn to own God's word for themselves. They have not really identified with it. My reflections and meditations are mine; they are the words that God seems to have spoken to me. Some people will identify with them, others will not, but I am absolutely certain that if we give God time, if we allow ourselves to be open to God's word, he can and will speak to each one of us.

10

The Bible is relevant to the world I live in

I have found the Psalms both inspirational and very relevant to my life. Turn to any psalm and we can discover what it has to say about us, about God, and about how, if we live as he wants us to, if we own that he is alive and interested in our lives, we can be the people he wants us to be.

The psalmist, David, didn't have a computer, but I do and sometimes it gives me a really bad time. So much so that I begin to feel that not just the computer but the whole of life is against me. I discovered that, even without a computer, the way David writes about life really identifies with where I am – and I discovered that God most surely is not against me.

I could catalogue a long list of things about computers that have gone wrong and got me down. Sometimes things do get us down. Sometimes we pretend that they don't. Sometimes we pretend that everything is just fine. But it's best not to pretend – with other people, or with God.

On one particular day I came in at 9.00 a.m. but my computer said it was 8.20 a.m. Then the whole thing seized up – and what's more it would not close down. So with a loud sigh I reset the thing and waited for it to do its stuff. Heyho, 9.10 a.m. That's better, Mr Computer. I can do without any hassle from you; lots to do, friends coming to lunch, shopping to do.

At the end of the morning I was just doing an important

piece of work when the call came for lunch. So, leaving my work open, I dashed off. On my return to the office it was time to go shopping, so I decided I'd better close down my work. I livened up the screen – and there was my precious work rushing down the screen over and over again and disappearing. I couldn't stop it. Click wherever – nothing worked. Eventually I managed to quit the programme. Things were definitely getting out of control.

Ah well, off to the shops. On my return I still had my work to finish – so I clicked the start button to open the last document, and the machine just closed itself down. Spooky.

I was really beginning to feel that the whole world was against me.

I can laugh a little now, but the truth is I'd been getting very frustrated with the computers; feeling that I'd got enough to do without constantly having to sort something out; feeling a bit angry with life, really. And, yes, feeling that the world was against me. Don't we all feel like that sometimes? Actually it's quite scriptural. We live in a fallen world. Things are not as they were meant to be. No wonder it's hard work at times.

But Jesus came to tell us that God is here with us. He has always been here. He is always the same. And he doesn't run away if we happen to be a bit grumpy. He sticks around and picks up the pieces and waits for us to say: "Hi Lord, thanks. I'm glad you're here with me."

If we read the Bible, particularly the Psalms, we find people who know exactly how we feel. Psalm 56 was written by David when he had been captured by the Philistines – at least, he had gone to see the king of Gath and then found that he was a prisoner. In order to escape he pretended to be a madman – and it worked.

He was also on the run from King Saul, so I guess he was having a pretty hassley time. And so he wrote Psalm 56 –

which reflects just how I had been feeling, and reminds me that actually God knows all about it.

Psalm 56 Living in the main beam

Please help me, Lord.
Life is just too much.
I can't keep up.
I'm hassled every time I turn round.
Computers,
The telephone,
I've forgotten to do this,
Someone wants something different.
I can't cope,
I'm scared.
But you, Lord, are there!
Just there!
Immovable!
Why should I be afraid
If you are there?

And you see it all, Lord.
You don't miss a thing
And you gather up my tears,
You keep a note of it all,
And you quietly say
"I'm on your side –
It's OK."

So what can happen to me?
Does it matter?
Nothing is as important
As you, Lord,

And my relationship with you.
What you really want me to do
Is to live as if you were by my side
Ready to pick me up when I fall.
You want me to live in the main beam
Not in the sidelights.
It's safe out in the main beam.
I can be seen
And then so can you.

Once again I had found that words written so long ago were relevant today – to the modern technological world that we live in. They can bring understanding and comfort, if only we slow down a bit and give them time to seep into our very being.

11

God is 100 per cent reliable

I was having an exciting time in the Psalms. Somehow the fact that someone living thousands of years ago had the same problems as me, and needed to learn the same lessons, was of more comfort than if someone round the corner or in the next pew had said the same thing. These words, written so long ago, were so up-to-date. Every picture was of a God who understood, who could be relied upon, who hadn't changed one iota in all that time.

This little psalm (71) was one of the first to "come at me" in different words and was a great encouragement to me not to give up on God, even when the going got tough.

Psalm 71:1–6 "I can take God at his word"

Lord –
You are 100 per cent reliable –
Don't ever give up on me.

Help me through the difficult times,
When life seems impossible.
I know that you hear me
And yet I need assurance.
Show me the right way forward.

Be my place of safety, Lord,
And draw me there often,
For you are the one who chose me,
Who showed me your way of life
And you have the power to keep me safe.

Keep me in the place
Where you want me,
With the people you want me to be with.

For you, Lord,
Are the most important person to me.
My future lies with you –
My past has been with you.

You have been present in my life
From the very beginning.
How amazing! –
That you were interested in me
Even then,
And had a plan for my life.
Thank you for your great and precious love and care.

As I began to learn more and more about this precious love and care that God has for me I was venturing into other parts of the Bible, particularly the Old Testament prophets, and, with a little more trepidation, the teachings of the New Testament.

PART TWO

Living the New Testament

12

You can *do it*

It was the Psalms that got me started on this voyage of discovery but I soon found that passages in the New Testament, too, could "come at me" in very different words. At first, I was a bit cautious because the New Testament writings are so different from the Old Testament, particularly the Psalms. The Psalms are very much about a heart response, whereas a great deal of the New Testament is teaching.

However, I soon discovered that it was really helpful to "get behind" some of the New Testament writings, and just think about them in relation to modern life, to expand on some of the thoughts. One of the first things I learnt was that I had some questionable preconceived ideas about Paul, who wrote many of the letters. I was in for a few surprises as I came to see Paul's writings in a different light.

Maybe, like me, you tend to think you are not clever enough to understand God's word and share it with others. But that's wrong. Maybe you think it was OK for the apostle Paul to be a great preacher, but you are inadequate. It's true that Paul was a very learned person, someone we might think of today as an academic. But he doesn't claim special eloquence or wisdom.

The following passage from his first letter to the Corinthians makes this very clear. But I hadn't really understood that until I "listened" to what Paul wrote and imagined him trying to find words to encourage his readers, and make them under-

stand that they had a responsibility to preach the word, too,
and that they were more than able to do so.

1 Corinthians 2:1–13 Believe me, it's worth believing

I haven't tried to tell you about God by using big words
And complicated ideas.
I am no more an expert on life than you are.
I don't have all the answers.
I only want to tell you about Jesus –
Jesus, who was crucified.

You maybe think I am crazy.
I certainly have been scared that you will think so.
And I have been frightened of saying the wrong thing.
I know that I cannot argue you into believing in Jesus.
And yet I so long for you to believe in him.
I have no long persuasive arguments,
No lengthy reasons why I think you should believe
    in God.
It is only God's Spirit who can speak to your heart
And convince you that God is who he says he is
And that Jesus is his Son who died for you.
But I do know
That if you believe this
You have to do something about it.
This can only happen
If God is allowed,
By his Spirit,
To work in your heart.

If I argue with you
And think that I have convinced you

That everything I know about Jesus is true,
I will have to spend the rest of my life
Convincing you to keep believing.
But if God's Holy Spirit works in your heart,
You will know for yourself
And your faith will be in God, not in me.

The message about Jesus
That we long to share
Is a difficult message to understand.
It doesn't make sense in today's world.
It doesn't cut any ice
With those who struggle to have wealth and power.
They don't realise
That all their wealth and power will come to nothing.

I was very excited when I read this passage and realised that, although Paul is often portrayed as someone who was too big for his boots, that does not really seem to be so. He was scared of what people would think but he was so sure of his message that he got on with the job, because he knew that the most important part of the job was not his – it was the Holy Spirit's. This reminded me of the very wise person who told me that if I persuaded people to *become* Christians, I would spend the rest of my life persuading them to *remain* Christians, which is probably why those words suddenly attached themselves to Paul's text.

I had thought I was familiar with this passage and knew what it said. Suddenly I found it saying lots of other things to me. I felt that I was just beginning to listen carefully, with an openness to God's word, ready to hear new things. It was as if there was secret writing underneath the typeface in my Bible, and every so often I would be able to see it and read it.

This passage left me feeling that the message is simple – we are the ones who make it complicated. It is also a message for today – in fact it could have been written today, it is so up-to-date.

13

God's grace – not our importance

Not only do we give too little time to reading the Bible, we do not give enough attention to God's grace. We do not realise that everything we have and do is by God's grace and, disgracefully, we often behave as if grace doesn't exist. We think that we are the clever, educated ones and have all the answers. We also often reject the person who is "different" and doesn't quite fit into our way of doing things. Jesus accepted everyone. We are very swift to condemn sin in others. He gently reminds us that he came to save sinners. We often behave as if we want to shut sinners out, forgetting that we are sinners ourselves.

Paul understood about the grace of God and he preached about it faithfully. He also realised that he could preach the gospel only by God's grace. This passage from Ephesians complements the passage in the previous chapter. Once again we find Paul putting himself down. This is quite a different picture from the one I have found in many books and heard from many preachers.

Ephesians 3:8–21 By God's grace

Am I better than anyone else?
Do I know more than anyone else?
Of course not!
I am not important.

64

But I do have a message that's important –
Not because I am any better than anyone else,
Nor do I have more grace than anyone else.
But because of God's grace in me.
It is only by this grace that I have a message.
Because this grace,
This message,
Is so wonderful,
I want to share it.

Somehow, by grace,
I know that God has created everything,
Including me.
And this is only because,
Somehow,
He has hidden this mystery within me.
He has opened up my heart
And Christ is in me.
This is such a great and wonderful truth
That I want to own Christ in others.
But how to do this?
It is such a mystery,
Yet we can all share in it.
And that is what God wants.
It is his plan
That we can come to him easily,
Confidently,
Because Jesus came to show us the way.
So I struggle
Because God's glory is for everyone,
And everyone needs to know that,
To experience it for themselves.

I can pray for you, my friends.
I acknowledge that God is the father of Jesus,
He is *my* father,
And he is *your* father.
I long for you to acknowledge him too.
I long
For God to open your hearts to himself
So that you begin to realise
How wonderful his glory is.
You can have this rich experience.
I long
For you to gain strength and purpose in your life,
Because you have given it to God.
I long
For the Holy Spirit
To help you believe
So that it is not just me owning Christ in you,
But you owning Christ for yourself.
His love needs to be the motivation
For all that you do.
You need to understand
A little of the love God has for you.
It's so enormous –
Impossible to measure.
It is beyond understanding.
God is so big
That when he fills you up
You'll feel fit to burst
With love for him
And others.
God can do this.
His glory
Can fill our lives

If we acknowledge him
Because he is glorious.

Someone once told me that the way he preached the gospel
was by "owning Christ in other people". I like that phrase,
"owning Christ in other people". It seems to me that this is the
most important thing we do, even when they have not owned
Christ in themselves. It is like an affirmation that enables God
to work in their lives. So often we do just the opposite –
instead of affirming, we condemn people; we make judgements about them, when we should be sharing God's grace
with them.

14

Secrets and mysteries

Have you ever tried to keep a secret? We read about mysteries in the Bible but they are not quite the same thing. A passage in Corinthians began to say quite a lot to me when I was trying to keep a secret from my husband, David, before he celebrated his 50th birthday. It can be very exciting when a passage you are reading from the Bible relates so closely to events that are occurring in your life at that moment. Not only did the passage set me thinking, but what was happening around me illustrated the truth of God's word.

My friend Ruth and I thought we would organise a surprise party. Now David is the most inquisitive person I know. He likes to know everything that is going on, and because I live and work with him it is very difficult to do things without him knowing. So keeping a secret from him was a nightmare, even though there was only a week to go before the party. Any longer and I would have become a nervous wreck – or a depressed heap.

I began to feel very anxious, and very "bad" about everything. Keeping a secret actually began to involve deceit and lies. This made me think about secrets and what they entail.

A secret can give you power – you know something
    others don't.
A secret can exclude people and make them feel left out.
A secret can cause suspicion and resentment.

The words "secret" and "hidden" are often used, all through the Bible. We sometimes talk of the "secret things of God". The feeling, always, is that one day all will be revealed and everyone will know the secret, hidden things of God. There is never a feeling of lies and deceit. Jesus suggests that there are those who won't get to know the secret. At first reading it looks as if they will not be allowed to know the secret, that it will be kept from them. But more likely Jesus meant it was because they have put themselves outside the circle of knowing what's going on. They are not ready to receive, therefore it will not be revealed to them. Those who are outside have set their own agenda and it is because of their disobedience that God's secret, or mystery, will not be revealed to them. It isn't that God doesn't want them to know.

God's secrets are probably better described as mysteries and they have to do with the truth which he longs for us to take on board, and act on in our lives. We will probably not know and understand most of God's mysteries until we get to heaven but I do think that God wants us to be always wanting to find out more. There is a sense in which we need to be as inquisitive as my husband, David. He is always wanting to know what's going on. Unlike me, struggling to keep from David the things that he wanted to know, God doesn't keep things from us. He longs to teach us new things if we are willing to learn.

Alongside all these thoughts about secrets and mysteries, I became fascinated with this little passage from 1 Corinthians 2, which talks about God's wisdom being a mystery which he reveals to us by his Holy Spirit – we cannot understand through our own brain power, but by relying on God's Holy Spirit working in our lives.

Part of David's inquisitiveness is about being in control. We all like to be in control, and that's often why we are unwilling to let a mystery be. But our search and enquiry needs to be in order to learn from God and rely on him, not in order to have power and control.

1 Corinthians 2:7–16 God's open secrets

We don't like to believe in things that we cannot see,
That we don't understand.
It makes us feel we are not in control.
This is why
The message that we have from God
Is difficult to share –
Difficult to understand.
We don't like to have a mystery –
We want to solve it.
But how can we know the whole of God's mystery?
It is totally beyond us.
It was always so throughout history.
We can read the writings from way back
And they say the same thing.

"It is impossible to comprehend
In any way
The rich store of good things
That God has planned for those of us who love him."

However, things are different now.
God has decided
That it is time we had a glimpse of these things
And so he has sent his Holy Spirit to help us.
To open the window a crack
So we can have an idea of what might be in store.

But we can only learn these things

Through the Spirit of God –
And that is mystery as well.
We do not know
Or understand
The things which are really important to another person,
The things which make him or her tick,
The things which motivate others.
We can never know
What goes on in the heart of someone else.
Indeed, at times
We hardly know what goes on inside ourselves.

How much more difficult
To know the deep things of God.
But his Spirit knows them well.
And God has given us his Holy Spirit,
So that we can begin to know more about him.
We have the Holy Spirit to teach us.

You would think then
That all would now be easy,
But it is not.
And why is this?
Because we are always flipping into human mode,
We keep turning off our communication with the Spirit,
And listening to ourselves.
We find it much easier
To look at the things that we can see and touch,
Listen to the words that other people speak,
And hear the clamour of the noisy world that we live in.

We need to push aside all those things,
Be quiet and listen to God.

For if we can begin to learn more about God,
Then we will grow more like him.
It *is* possible to do this.

This is a good example of how, if we allow our thoughts
enough room, we can find a lesson from God's word through
something happening in our own life (in this case a significant
birthday celebration). Keeping hold of the things that God
shows us can be quite difficult. We need to keep reminding to
ourselves, if we are to live our lives in the light of the lessons
learnt and not return to our old ways. I find I can remember
some of the lessons I learnt from God's word by this kind of
association with an important event, some occasion that I
often recall.

15

Setting our minds to things

God wants us to set our minds to things. If we consider how Jesus set his face like flint towards Jerusalem, towards the cross, towards fulfilling God's purpose, nothing we have to do is that difficult. Yet we *do* find it hard, and we have to rely upon God to help us when we feel like giving up. We have to be determined.

This doesn't come naturally to me – I easily give up. My very first venture into hearing a passage in the New Testament "come at me" in different words was when I was reading the first chapter of 1 Peter. "Make up your mind" (verse 13) was a phrase which made me sit up and listen. I am not very good at making my mind up and getting on with it. I am more of a ditherer. Actually allowing the New Testament to impact on our lives and change them is a bit scary. But it was verse 14 which stopped me in my tracks: "As obedient children, do not conform to the evil desires you had when you lived in ignorance." To be obedient to God we have to be pretty determined – it's much easier to go our own way. So I started to read the section again, and I began to write.

1 Peter 1:13–25 Living the way God wants

Make up your mind
And be determined not to give up.

Be sensible.
Stake everything you have
On the fact that God loves you –
You know this is true.
It's as if he's given you a cheque
And when Jesus comes again
You'll be able to cash it in full.
Wow!
Think about what you are doing
And get it right.
OK, so you used not to give God much space in your life
And if you hurt people,
Did things you knew were wrong,
You thought, "Who cares?"
You were enjoying yourself.
Surely you're allowed to enjoy yourself?
Now you know better –
God wants you to be like him –
OK, so you won't get it right all the time
But you need to try.
You need to think about how you behave,
Consider the things you do,
How they affect others,
What God thinks about it.

What if Jesus was right there by your side?
Well, he is!
And he is the Holy One,
God.
God's word says
"Be holy, for I am holy."
OK, that's pretty impossible
But it doesn't mean we give up.

We need to make a few deposits in our account now
So that when Jesus does come
We will be holy
Because we'll be able to draw on our account
With all the interest.
If you are really calling God Father
Then you need to think about how you are living.
You are on a journey
And one day you'll arrive
Then you'll have to account for how you got there.
Remember you are precious to God
Not because of anything
Except that Jesus died for you.
He died in your place –
He was the perfect one.
He died to give you the opportunity to be perfect.
And what a long time it all takes.

Before the world began
This was all planned.
So you must have been important then.
And now he's shown it all to you.
You know that Jesus died,
You know that he is risen.
God has done this.
This is the God you are dealing with.
He's given you the opportunity to be his friend,
To live your life alongside him.

Once again I found myself blown away by these words. They really hit home, to the depths of my being. Imagining Jesus by my side in every situation made me very ashamed. Thinking about all that was on offer from God, and asking myself what

I was doing about it – that was quite mind-blowing.

Was this really what this passage was saying? Is this what Peter was saying? And why was it that these words made it much more relevant to me? It is so easy to think that the Bible is just a book of rules, given to make sure we don't enjoy ourselves. If we have that mindset, we won't be very keen to read it – it might tell us things we don't want to know; it might demand things that we don't want to give.

Yet even though this passage is challenging, I don't find it threatening. I thought that God's word would keep condemning the way I live my life, lots of serious stuff telling me off. But this is not what I have discovered. Rather, the Bible seems to understand exactly how I feel. Can a book understand you? Well of course it is *God* who understands us, and it's as if by allowing myself to get behind the words on the page, *they read me as I read them*.

16

Never give up

We can all make resolutions and be determined to do something, but once the initial inspiration or encouragement has faded, it's easy to get bogged down. Paul tells us we must not lose heart, we must not give up.

This next passage hit a very tender spot. It reminded me that I know only too well what I should be doing, but I make all kinds of excuses not to. Once more I became excited as God seemed to speak directly to me, telling me a few home truths about myself.

2 Corinthians 4:1–18 Don't lose heart

We know what we should be doing,
And we must not give up
Or feel overwhelmed,
Because all the help and encouragement we need
Is at hand.

We need to stand up and be counted,
Speaking out against what we know to be wrong,
Not pretending to go along with the crowd
Because they might think we're a bit old-fashioned
    or pious.
We need to own that Jesus is important in our lives.

If people don't seem to hear us,
Or ignore what we are saying,
As long as we have not been afraid
To own the truth of God's love in our lives,
We have done all we can.
Sometimes people are totally blinded
To any thought of God
Because they are so wrapped up in the world
And all they think it has to offer.

Sometimes it is hard
For God to penetrate the darkness
That surrounds people.
He doesn't burst into people's lives
When they don't want him to.
We, like him,
Have to be patient and faithful,
Making sure that we constantly reflect the love of Jesus.

Remember,
It is the God who caused the light
To shine out through the darkness
Who shone this light into our hearts.
It is a powerful light that shows us Jesus and his love.

If only we were bright and shining silver,
How we would reflect his light;
It would positively sparkle from us.
But alas, we are dull and dark.
All the glory and power are God's.

Once we realise this

It gives our failures a new perspective.
Yes, life is tough,
Pressing in on us from every direction,
But we won't be suffocated.

Yes, we are confused
By all the different messages that come at us
Pulling us this way and that,
But we don't need to give up.

Yes, we may feel that we are ridiculed
And made fun of,
But we are not alone.

Yes, we may stumble and fall over,
But we can get up again.
Because Jesus is in us,
In our very being,
We can experience a little of his dying,
And we can experience a little of his living.
In fact, it is only as we take on board his death,
That we truly experience his life.

Jesus didn't promise an easy life.
We need to experience difficulty
In order to appreciate his love for us.
We do not have an empty faith –
We have something to tell others about.

And we know that
Just as Jesus was raised to life,
So we are raised above the difficulties of this present life,
And one day we will be raised up to heaven.

And what a lot we will have to give thanks for
As we meet together.

So don't lose heart, don't give up.
Life may be difficult,
We may grow weary
We may grow old,
But that is just our outer selves, our "shell".
The real you, the real me, is being renewed day by day,
Being brought closer to God.
What is happening now
Is so insignificant
Compared to the moment
When we meet Jesus in heaven
And experience the total glory of God.

It's hard to imagine the unseen –
Eternity is a long way away from our experience,
But that is actually what is real.

"Stand up and be counted," I wrote. I remind myself of that phrase, often. It's hard to do that, but God will help us. The thought of being a powerful reflector of his love to the people around should be enough encouragement to make us all stand up and be counted.

17

Satan is a subtle fellow

Satan is a subtle fellow and, since most of us find it difficult to talk about him as if he really exists, he's got an open invitation to be busy in our lives. Satan is able to make life difficult for us without our noticing who is responsible. I think of the story Jesus told about the weeds growing up even though the seed that had been sown was good. The reason is that an enemy has stealthily sown the bad seeds among the good ones. "An enemy has done this" (Matthew 13:28).

Sometimes bad things happen to us, or things don't work out very well. It is easy to blame ourselves and wonder what we have done wrong. We are puzzled because we don't see any solution, any way of improving things, and it really does seem as though there is some evil influence at work which we can't understand.

It reminds me of the beginning of the book of Job, where God asks Satan what he's been up to. Satan replies that he's just been wandering up and down, roaming around the earth. I can imagine him doing just that, on the lookout for where he can sow some discontent, upset things, make things difficult, confuse people, cause them to doubt what they know to be true.

Wherever there is great potential for God's Spirit to be at work, we would be wise to beware. Satan will not be at all happy about it and he will be trying to make things difficult for God's children.

It would help if it was obvious to us when Satan is meddling in things, but he is much too subtle for that. One of the easiest places for Satan to cause mayhem is in relationships. Our relationships are very precious and very fragile. If Satan can convince us that we don't agree with each other, and generally stir up trouble, he can distract us from noticing that he is doing anything at all.

When life is a struggle, we easily get discouraged, but in fact our struggle can be a reason to be encouraged. Satan isn't going to bother causing trouble where there's no need. However, if the Spirit of God is at work in people's lives, if there is a potential for God's word to be heard by people, beware! Satan will be worried. In other words, if life gets tough, we probably have good reason to praise God.

If we are frightened of Satan and his devious ways, Ephesians 6:10–18 offers us encouragement. We have at our disposal a whole suit of armour from God and it will enable us to have the victory. All the protection God offers is available to us – but it's not an easy set of armour to put on. It takes effort on our part. It's not the kind of armour you can slip inside and hide. You need to put it on boldly and stride forth, confidant that God will not let you down, and that Satan will retreat.

Ephesians 6:10–18 Know the enemy

We need to realise
Just how powerful God is –
Beyond our comprehension –
And claim all that power for our very own.
We need to claim everything
That is available to us from God
If we are going to beat the devil at his wiley games.

He is so cunning and subtle

He makes us think
That our troubles are because of other people,
He stirs up our relationships,
He makes us struggle against each other,
He confuses us.

The reality is,
We struggle against things we barely understand,
That, often, we don't admit exist.
Only God understands these things,
Knows how to deal with them
And has the resources available for us to deal with
    them, too.
The battles rage in heaven over our very souls,
And we need all the protection God has to offer
So that when we finally meet God in heaven
We shall be untainted by the evil which is ever near us,
Prowling round, looking for our weak points.

Hang on to the truth –
Don't let it become corrupted –
Don't let it be added to or watered down.
If Jesus is our righteousness
Then God looks at us
And sees Jesus
And loves us,
And Satan cannot persuade us otherwise.
His lies cannot affect us.

Make sure you walk the way of peace,
Always carrying the good news with you,
Always ready to share it,
Going where God leads.

And most important,
Believe that God is who he says he is,
And has done the things he has said he has done.
For then no seeds of doubt can be sown in your heart –
Don't let them get past your guard.

For you have been saved by the precious blood of Jesus.
You are his,
You belong to him,
And one day you will be with him for ever
In the place that he has prepared especially for you.

And remember,
The word of God is like a sword,
Make sure you read it,
You know it,
You can use it.
You never know when you will need it.

Talk to God,
Spend time with him,
Get to know him
And his Spirit will help you.

Be ever mindful of his presence and his power.
Ask for help.
Pray for one another.
Don't give up.
Be on your guard.
Be a good watchman.
Be ready.

18

Lighten up – it's OK

This next passage is very precious to me.

I didn't really want to write down the things that came to me as I read it. It's such a familiar passage and somehow I seemed to be changing the words too much and maybe changing the sense. But I just had to write it down. In fact, for some reason I tucked a copy of it into my Bible. Not long afterwards there came an occasion when a group of us were struggling with difficult and painful issues and the tears were flowing and I knew that I needed to read it. God was saying to us "It's OK!" We could hardly believe it – but he was right.

Later I learnt that the sense of those first words "Rejoice, and again I say rejoice" in their original language meant very much "it's OK". I was astounded. I also felt that God was giving me a precious token of his love and a very big hug. In fact that was what he was giving to us all.

Philippians 4:4–8 It's OK, really!

Lighten up! It's OK. God knows.
You can relax. Let go. Let God.
Just let him know about it.
It will be all right.
What a wonderful feeling
Of peace and comfort comes over us.

We just know
That Jesus is there.
He will not let us go.
He will keep us safe.

So keep your mind in gear
And think about the things that are important.
Get your priorities right
And don't be distracted.
Whatever the situation
Don't be misled.
Walk tall.
Don't grovel in the gutter.
Do the right thing, even when it hurts.
Don't let your mind be poisoned
By idle gossip, or bad language.
Look for the good things,
The beautiful things in life
And in people's lives around you.
Have good things to say,
Positive things.
Be encouraging.

Those last verses (8–9) have always fascinated me. They often come to mind when I've read or watched something on television which has filled my mind with horrible things. The Authorized Version of the Bible uses those beautiful words "Whatsoever things are true, whatsoever things are noble," etc. It's a timely reminder to think on the things of God. So I was even more comforted to have a few thoughts filled out for me, as it were. I was glad to be reminded that I need to make an effort to encourage, that I have a responsibility to affirm other people.

19

A second chance

I often feel as though I have been given a second chance with reading God's word. I have come such a long way from that young, scared Christian who was frightened of saying the wrong thing, and easily persuaded that maybe I wasn't a Christian after all. Then, when people talked about the excitement of reading God's word, I didn't really understand what they meant – to me it was very much a book of rules, an instruction manual. It is those things, but so much more and, if we are willing to have a heart response to it, who knows what will happen. It took me twenty years to let God enlighten me.

Once we accept Jesus as our friend and Saviour it is easy to think that we've arrived. Nothing is further from the truth. It took our patient God ages of time to bring his plan to fruition in Jesus. Although this passage is about what God has done for us in Jesus, it is, for me, a truth I have had to learn over and over.

1 Peter 1:3–9 God never gives up

God never gives up, does he?
Even though first time round we messed it up big time;
All his plans for us
We threw back in his face.
To all the things he wanted to give us

We said *"No thanks!*
We can sort it all out ourselves.
We can get what we want without you, God!"

How wrong we were!
And how badly wrong it all went!
So God tries again in another way.
And this time –
Nothing can spoil it,
Nothing can change it,
Nothing can overcome it.
Because this time his gift to us
Is his Son
Jesus.

How can we say *"No!"* again?
Because this time he is our only hope.
He has *died* to sort it all out.
And because he is alive again
It *is* sorted.
What can be greater than that?
So start singing – now.
And keep singing.
Even though life will still get tough.
After all, Jesus suffered,
So how can we expect to do otherwise?
But keep singing
Because you *will* get there in the end.
It *will* all be worthwhile.
This time nothing will keep you from all that God wants to
    give you.
Even though you can't quite see it,
Even though you don't have all the answers,

When Jesus comes
To take you to himself
And give you your rightful place,
All the hassle will be as nothing.
You will be so glad that you survived the trauma.
You will have grown in stature
And, best of all,
You love
And are loved by
God himself.
You realise you could never have sorted it yourself.
How great that God was willing
For there to be
A second time round.

Sometimes I think there are many times round for us all. We
continually need to come back to the truth of this passage and
renew our commitment.

20

Keeping in touch

We need to keep in touch.

Communication is so immediate now and so easy. How did we ever cope without email? It's transformed our lives. It makes communication a completely different ball game, and what importance we attach to it! We must have our mobile, to be in communication at all times! Telephones are not just for home and the office. They are for when we're walking down the road, driving the car. Whatever we are doing and wherever we are we must be able to communicate, whether it's business, or friends, or just because we have forgotten something. We feel we can't operate unless we are at the end of a phone or shooting emails off all over the world with replies coming so quickly that it is almost like using the phone.

But do we dial in to God as regularly? We don't really operate properly if we don't communicate with God. How important do we rate prayer? Can we survive without prayer? Do we make sure we're on line with God?

God just longs to listen to us; he knows that is how we operate best – in communication with him. Paul wrote about this to the Christians in Colossae. He told them that God had opened the lines of communication – all they had to was use them.

Colossians 1:19–23 Jesus has mended the broken line

Everything we need is to be found in Jesus.
That's how God planned it.
And that's the way it is.
Why?
Because God wants to be able to chat to you.
He wants the lines of communication to be open.
That's why Jesus had to die on the cross –
To mend the broken lines of communication.
God knows that you want to run away from him.
He knows you're frightened
That you might have to give something up if you listen
    to him.
He knows you keep turning your back on him
Because you are selfish and want to do your own thing.
You want to please yourself – not God.
He knows all that.
He knows about all that rejection.
And yet –
The communication is there ready for you.
You just have to dial in
And the death of Jesus makes everything OK;
And his resurrection means
You can plug in to all the power that God has available.
Gigabytes have nothing on the power of God.
You have heard all this before and you know it is true.
You know it's there for you.

So go live – get on line to God. Tap into all that power. If
communicating with your friends is important, it has to be
important to communicate with God. Communication is
everything in this busy world. If we miss a call we get so

agitated. Do you rush in and dial 1471? Do you hurry to interrogate the answerphone? Do you check your emails the minute you get near your computer? Maybe you should worry more about missing a call from God. That's where the real power is.

21

Why so hard?

With all these exciting discoveries, I began to wonder why we find it difficult to read the Bible. These are some of my thoughts as I considered how much more difficult the Old Testament seemed than the New, yet how worthwhile it was to explore it.

As a child I heard all the Bible stories over and over again. But today people don't have a bank of stories from the Bible tucked away at the back of their minds because they heard them all in junior school or Sunday school.

We may be Christians, but most of us don't read the Bible every day. Sometimes we only listen to it being read when we go to church. We don't give ourselves much opportunity to find out more from the Bible but just let it glance off us. Is that because we live in an "instant coffee" type of world, where everyone expects quick and easy answers that do not require much effort? The advertising that is constantly thrust at us gives the message – "you can have what you want, no effort required".

I am no different from anyone else. If I read a passage of the Bible that is difficult, I find it hard to persevere. I don't really want to spend time delving into the original Hebrew or Greek languages that the Bible was written in; I don't want to read the history of the time, or even what someone else has written about the passage.

But one day, when I was reading a passage in Isaiah 29 which I really didn't understand at all, this verse popped out at me: "In that day the deaf shall hear the words of the book, and the eyes of the blind shall see out of obscurity and out of darkness."

This seemed to suggest that much in the Bible would seem obscure and difficult to understand. Either Isaiah or God himself understood how I felt! The prophet seemed to be saying that life wouldn't always be difficult, the things of God would not always be shrouded in mystery: one day all will be revealed. The trouble is, I want everything to be easy now, this minute. I don't want to waste time reading the instructions. I just want to get on as quickly as possible.

God says that we *will* understand eventually and, meanwhile, we need to do our best to get to know him. We do need to read the instructions. He longs for us to understand his word, he longs to help, but there are so many reasons why we remain hungry and don't understand, or even hear, what he says to us. I think this verse says that God will find a way.

So, as I tried to gather my thoughts, I wrote a psalm of my own, expressing some of my frustrations. I hope you may be able to identify with them.

My personal psalm

Your word is hard to understand, Lord.
Even Christians close their minds to it.
If it doesn't immediately make sense,
If it's not easily understood,
If it doesn't seem relevant straight away,
Then it is pushed aside.
But if we don't try to understand your word,
How can we expect people who don't know you to try?

I know your word can speak to my soul.
I don't understand how,
But I have to be open to that possibility.
I need to be open for that to happen.
Sometimes I know that you have spoken deep within me
But I cannot put it into words; I can't explain it.

Don't let me miss the wonder and marvel of all you want
   to show me
Because I am in too much of a hurry.

In our world of instant coffee and instant news,
Our world of science, technology and
   understanding things,
It is easy to close our minds,
And so our hearts and souls, to what God is saying.
We want the answer without any effort on our part,
We think everything should be explained by our own
   scientific knowledge,
We are not comfortable with mysteries.

Open my mind to every possibility.
Open my understanding to the unexplainable.
Open my heart to the deep yearnings of your heart, Lord.
Help me to make an effort –
To be willing to spend time trying;
To be willing to wait for an answer;
To be willing to wait for *your* answer
And not just make up my own.

I have tried to make this last verse my prayer. I have tried to be
open to all that God wants me to have. But I confess it is hard
sometimes. It is hard to find time. It is hard to be in the mood.

It is hard to concentrate. It is hard to be open. It is hard, *but it is worth it*.

It really is important for all of us to read the Bible for ourselves. It is not enough to listen to the readings in church on Sundays, to hear what the preacher says about it. Going to the mid-week Bible Study isn't enough, either. These are all good things to do – but not enough.

The Bible is about God, about Jesus, but it is also about you and me. As we read it we find that it is able to read us. As we read its story we find that it becomes our story. If we are willing to spend a little time, even those really obscure bits of the Bible have the potential to jump out and say something quite unexpected. It *is* possible to understand and own passages from the Old Testament, and I have certainly been very surprised by some of the things I have found there, especially in passages that were so familiar I thought I already knew what they meant.

22

Getting to grips with the difficult bits

I have always found the prophets difficult and complicated. I felt they needed a lot of study to understand what was going on. They seem to switch around from speech to description, from God speaking to the prophet speaking, and it is difficult to keep up. It is a bit like reading a script in which you have no idea who is saying what – or why they are saying it. Isaiah is a good example – a very long book with long chapters, quite a bit of it written in verse. There are some passages which are quite familiar, especially if you have listened to Handel's *The Messiah*. But much of it is very difficult to follow.

I was surprised to find myself fascinated by a passage in chapter 58. It is about fasting, a subject with which we are not so familiar these days. I vividly remember an occasion when a group of us were talking about fasting and someone said that they tried to fast on Fridays. I will never forget the response from someone else in the group who said that he always thought fasting was like going on hunger strike – "I won't eat another bean until you give me what I want, Lord."

Reading this passage in Isaiah I realised that here were some other folk who hadn't quite got the right idea about fasting. So much so, that God felt someone would have to do some shouting if folk were to actually hear what he wanted to say to them. He had to have someone shout for him.

Isaiah 58:1–11 Tell it the way it is

Shout it to the rooftops,
Give it all you've got.
Tell it the way it really is.
Yes, my people seek me.
Yes, they seek my ways.
Yes, they want my justice.
They delight to seek after me.
But –
They fast begrudgingly,
Saying,
"Why haven't you heard me, God?
Why haven't you answered, Lord?"
They think their fasting hurts them
And I take no notice.
In fact
Their fasting is an excuse.
They have their own agenda,
Their own reasons for fasting.
No wonder I do not hear.
The fast I have chosen
Is a different way.
It's a hard way
And it will hurt.
It will cost.
I long
For you not to be bound up with evil things.
I long
For you not to be restricted and bound by your own evil
    desires,
The burdens of your own making.
I long

For you to enjoy freedom.
And you can play a part in this –
But it will cost you.

You need to share your wealth with the poor.
You need to share what I have given you,
The chosen,
With those who are rejected and unloved.
You need to open your eyes
To other people's circumstances,
Not close your eyes
And pretend you do not see.

Then your life will be meaningful.
It will light up.
You will have much more to offer.
Your life will be real
And there will be something of my presence with you.
Then I will hear and answer you.

Stop blaming others for what is your own fault.
You are the chosen ones,
It is your place to obey,
To open up your very soul.
Then your light will shine:
There will be no darkness.
I will show you the way,
I will satisfy you,
I will give you strength,
And you will grow.
There will be no going back.

Here is God telling Isaiah to give everyone the wake-up call –
give them a bit of a lecture, because they really weren't doing
what God required of them at all. These days we don't seem
very clued up about fasting, but in Isaiah's time people were,
so they ought to have got it right.

I didn't understand very much about fasting – it wasn't
something that I had tried. But this passage really challenged
me, because it seemed to be about hypocrisy; it seemed to be
about the cost of pleasing God; it seemed to be about my
responsibility to do something about injustices. And it was
also about God's promise never to let me down.

23

God's surprises

When I allow God's word to "come at me", when I spend time being open to what God has to say, when I slow down and relax, that's when I find that God's word surprises me most. Did you know it was OK to have a grumble at God and tell him how you really feel?

There are three guys in the Old Testament who really encourage me – not because of their great faith; not because they were always worshipping God; not because they always found life a breeze; not because they basked in God's sunshine and were always telling people how God was blessing them; not because life was just perfect for them. No, they encourage me because they had a go at God when life was difficult and they were wondering if God was really there. They had a good moan – and it was OK!

The first is Job. I had always thought that he was a long-suffering fellow God reckoned he could let Satan play fast and loose with, and Job would still come up trumps. I thought Job just kept his head down until it was all over, told his friends off when they tried to comfort him, and insisted that he had done nothing wrong. Well, he did do those things, but that's not all.

Job 23 Grumpy me!

Well, I'm in a right grump today.
All I can do is moan.
I'm so fed up I can't be bothered to do anything.
I'd like to tell God just how I feel.
If I knew he was listening, I'd tell him a thing or two.
Why can't I find him?
I *would* listen to what he had to say –
In fact I think it is time he gave me a few answers.

But, no matter how hard I try, I can't seem to find him.
It's as if he's hiding from me, deliberately not listening.
It's hard to hang in there;
It's hard to believe this is all for my own good.
I've tried so hard – I thought I was doing all right –
But it all seems to have gone horribly wrong.

I guess he knows what he is doing,
I have to trust he's got it all under control,
But I'm so scared.
You would think he'd keep the darkness from me,
But he hasn't and I am so frightened.
I hardly dare believe, and yet I know that he is God,
Almighty God!
And he is working out his plan for me.

Have you ever felt like that? That you were trying your best but felt absolutely dreadful and that God was a long way away. Job had every reason to be grumpy. God didn't seem to be interested, even though Job had such a close relationship with God. He had followed all the rules. He'd tried to please God. And yet here he was, really suffering, having lost everything that was dear to him. Yes, he had every reason to be grumpy.

Somehow I don't think I have quite the same excuse. Yet sometimes I feel so grumpy, and even though I try to reason with myself, even though I can't see why I'm being grumpy when I should really be counting my blessings, I still can't get my act together. God doesn't seem to be there. It's as if I am praying to the ceiling. I begin to feel cross with God and wonder why he doesn't sort it all out.

That's how I was feeling when I read this passage: God was not listening to me. And suddenly here was Job expressing my feelings exactly. So I came to the conclusion that God does care, he is there beside us even though we don't realise it. Yet I still go on being scared, because I need to wait to feel better about things.

Why do we rely on our feelings so much? It's a good thing God understands.

My next encourager is Jeremiah. What a very morose fellow he is, and how difficult it is to understand his writings. A few passages of Jeremiah are well known and we tend to ignore the rest. To my shame, I was speed-reading through Jeremiah when suddenly a passage in chapter 20 stopped me in my tracks. Jeremiah was having a good grumble, and it seemed to me that it was a perfectly healthy thing to do. After all, God knows how we *really* feel, so there is not much point in keeping quiet and pretending that we are all right.

Here Jeremiah tells God just how frustrated he is. He really feels he's done his bit about things – so why isn't God keeping his end of the bargain?

Jeremiah 20:7–18 "You've dropped me in it, Lord"

Lord, I did what you said
And where has it got me?
Everyone thinks I'm a freak.
How much easier it would be
To ignore you,
Not mention you any more.
But how can I keep quiet?
Your word is burning inside me.
I know it is true.
I may be silent for a while
But then I can stand it no longer,
I have to speak out.

And then I wish I hadn't.
Everyone looks at me
As if I've said something wrong
I can feel them talking about me
Behind my back
And I wish I could shrink into the ground.

OK Lord, I know you are there.
I know your message is true.
I know that they won't have the last laugh.
But couldn't you shut them up now?
They make my life so miserable.
I wish I'd never been born.
Life is just too difficult.

When I read that, a friend had just been telling me that she
was fed up with being a Christian because it made her different from her friends. How great it would be not to be

considered some kind of freak all the time. Life seemed so difficult. Well, I knew how she felt, and so did Jeremiah.

Encourager number three is King David, in a little psalm he wrote when he was in total despair, sure that God was there, but unable to find him, and feeling that God really ought to respond.

Psalm 142 "Please help – life's scarey"

Are you there, Lord?
Do you realise how miserable I am?
I need you to know that.

It's very scarey when life is black.
I just despair; I feel I am totally alone.
Surely, Lord, you know how it's been for me.
I really don't think anyone loves me
Or appreciates what I do.
I always seem to get things wrong.
I feel so abandoned.

You are my only hope, Lord,
I don't have anyone else to turn to.
I know that you can help,
But just at the moment
I feel trapped, unable to find you,
And I'm only just hanging on.
My only hope is that eventually you will rescue me.

David was a great king, and an important person in the ancestry of Jesus. Jerusalem itself, the city of God, is also named after him "the city of David". Yet even he felt abandoned by God, so it is little wonder if we sometimes feel that way too.

So where is the happy ending? Where is God? After all, if we are Christians, if we believe God is there, he will surely come up trumps – won't he?

In these passages from Job, Jeremiah and David, we don't actually find the answer to the complaints – and sometimes that's what happens to us. We can't quite get the answer or the assurance we need. Just like Job or Jeremiah or David, we can't get beyond our feelings. Fortunately, if we read on from each of these passages we can see that things do change for all three. But if we were in their shoes – Job stuck in chapter 23, Jeremiah stuck at verse 18 in chapter 20, and David at the end of Psalm 142 – life would have seemed pretty dire, and we too would have felt we had every right to complain.

Maybe we *do* have a right to complain at times when we are in that sort of situation. The fact that the Bible includes these complaints means it's OK to feel this way sometimes and it's OK to tell God about it. As long as we don't get stuck there. Having got things off our chest we need to move on in our lives.

I am sure that if we are honest with God he is able to bless. Remember Jesus' disciple Thomas – usually labelled doubting Thomas – in the New Testament? When Thomas complained that he couldn't possibly believe Jesus had risen from the dead unless he saw him for himself, we might have expected Jesus to be cross about his lack of faith and disappointed in him. Actually Jesus' response was to give Thomas a very special experience of himself. How must Thomas have felt as he was allowed to touch Jesus in the very places that he was so wounded? We too must open up, allow ourselves to be vulnerable, and God will bless us.

Similarly, if we open ourselves to God's word, he is able to bless us by taking us behind the words, filling in the feelings and telling us that he understands.

24

God's word reads me

The Psalms form the heart of the Bible. As well as being in the middle, they contain a personal heart response to God. They also contain some wonderful wisdom about God's word, and about God. They are encouraging and uplifting, they are honest and we can identify with their words so easily. Perhaps that's why I started there with my response to God's word. Psalm 119 has a great deal to say about God's word and encouraged me as God's word puts life back into perspective for me.

The place where I was when I began to write God's word a little differently – flat on my face! – was probably a good place to start. Many of the psalms start there, too, and move us on to understanding and knowing God more. So do other parts of the Old Testament. They also reveal a God who is very close to us, identifies with us and understands how we feel. Just like Job, Jeremiah and David I was discovering again and again how very up-to-date what we read in the Bible is. It is exciting to read these words, as true today as they were when they were written. So here is just a reminder that God has always been "cool", before we move on to some other parts of the Old Testament.

Psalm 73 God is cool!

I know that God is God
But it sure ain't cool to think that way.
My friends all think I'm a freak.
They all seem to be OK;
They have no worries.
They bounce along through life
From one party to the next,
Doing what they like.
They always seem to have plenty of money,
Fast cars, nice clothes;
And they have no thought for others,
Those begging on the streets,
Those out of work,
Those who are starving –
Just not their problem.
They've no time for God at all –
They have all the answers they need.
If all their wishes were prayers, God seems to have
    answered them.
What about *my* prayers, Lord?
It seems I go to all this trouble
To try and do what you want,
Go to church, read my Bible, say my prayers.
And where does it get me?
I stand up for you and where does it get me?
Nothing but grief.
I just can't make it all add up.

So here I am again, Lord,
Reading your word,
Seeking your face.

And then you show it me the way it really is:
They act big and confident;
But that's all an act.
They look as if they are on the way up;
But in fact their feet are on the slippery slope downwards.
They think that possessions and having a good time are
    all-important;
But actually they fear that they might not keep up.
I'm sorry, Lord.
I am totally rich in comparison.
And I need to keep trying to share the reason why,
And *not* give up.
They want to know about you really.
And how could I doubt that you have got things in hand
    for me?
How could I think that you'd forgotten me,
That you were ignoring me,
And that my friends were better off
Because they didn't have to consider what you wanted
    of them?

You are the greatest!
And you are not just in heaven,
You are here on earth.
And I want to be with you here on earth
As well as in heaven.
Without you I fail, full of doubt and fear,
And, yes, resentment.
But with *you* my heart is full of love
And I am strangely confident.

God doesn't think we're freaks. Once again I was brought back
into line as God's word read me, showed me where I was, and

encouraged me on my way. Reading the Bible was worth every minute, trying to follow what God wanted for me was worth it and this included delving into the Old Testament.

25

Blown away!

When I'm least expecting it, and probably when I need it most, I feel as though I have been completely blown away by what I read in God's word. I thought I knew the story of Jonah fairly well. I wondered how he could be so stupid as to think that he could escape from God. I thought God must be very fed up with him, and a little short on patience. I suppose it shows a sense of humour on God's part that he allowed Jonah to be swallowed by a big fish. It had never occurred to me before that I was often rather like Jonah and could be a candidate for the same treatment!

Jonah must have felt completely abandoned and isolated. I can't quite imagine what it must be like to be inside the stomach of a large creature: dark, wet, confusing. Jonah probably thought his time was up. He knew that he had disobeyed God and that God was responsible for his present condition. God had obviously had enough and that was the end of the matter. So Jonah has a last shout at God, not really believing he will hear – and Jonah gets a bit of a surprise. He finds that God is listening, and not only listening, but that he still cares about Jonah and what is happening to him.

Jonah 2:1–9 "I love you"

What on earth am I doing here, Lord?
What's that?
You can hear me down here?
Well, that's amazing –
I thought I'd sunk too far.
For I seem to be in the very depths;
As low as I can be.
I seem to be completely out of your sight.
I guess I thought I'd really blown it this time,
That there was no way back.
I'd shut you out just one time too many,
I'd left you out.
I'd been disobedient – again –
And gone my own way,
Ignoring you,
Forgetting you,
And I deserved to be forgotten by you.
Struggling in the dark,
Entangled in all the wretched things of life that I
    thought I wanted,
I thought the prison bars had clanged shut
And that you'd thrown away the key.
In my desperation I called to you
But I thought it was too late.
I remembered the good times
And I thought they'd gone for ever.
I'd given up, Lord.
I didn't think you'd bother any more.
And then you spoke:
"I love you.
No matter what you do, I love you."

What lovingkindness you have for me, O God
And not just for me.
No wonder you want me to tell others
To turn away from all the things which distract them
    from you,
From the little gods they worship.
Well, I will do what you want, Lord.
I promise.

I got a bit of a surprise too. Because just as I thought God was saying "I love you" to Jonah – I realised that he was saying "I love you" to me as well. I found the tears pouring down my face as I realised that no matter how disobedient I am, no matter how many times I let God down, or turn away from him, he still loves me.

I had started out by feeling a bit superior to Jonah – I'd never be as stupid as him. I ended up realising that I could never come up to Jonah's stature but, even so, God was still saying to me too, "I love you". We may be trying to escape from God, like Jonah, or we may find ourselves feeling that we've really blown it and God must certainly have given up on us. We need to realise, along with Jonah, that God never gives up on us and he never stops loving us.

Interestingly this passage spoke to me in this way just before I specially needed to know that God loved me. It meant that I was able to face the subsequent events in my life in a way that would have been impossible otherwise. Yes, I suppose I did know that God loved me, but somehow this was a very special word that provided me with new strength and assurance.

26

Riding the thermals

Isaiah 40:28–31 is another passage from the Old Testament that was a source of great encouragement to me. When you are weary and discouraged, flat on your face, it's hard to imagine taking to the skies and rising above everything. It is hard to imagine you could soar above things when you've hardly the energy to drag yourself up the stairs to bed. It's good to know that God never gets tired. It's also good to be reminded that if we are so very weary it may be time to take stock and re-organise our priorities. There's a good chance we have been trusting in our own strength, and it's when we get to the end of our strength that we can be borne up by God's strength.

Isaiah 40:28–31 Soaring like eagles

Don't you realise that God never gets tired?
And, amazingly, he never gives up on us.
He knows just what we are like.
And when we give up
He picks us up.
We always start off with so much enthusiasm
Lots of energy,
Thinking we can do everything.

But even the youngest, the most energetic,

Will eventually run out of strength.
All that's left is God.
If we ask,
He will give all that we need
In abundance.
Have you ever watched the eagles?
Imagine rising up above the mountain,
Soaring above everything,
Riding the thermals.

Well, that's what it's like when God takes over.
If we thought we once had energy,
We are now supercharged.
If we thought we were once strong,
We are now bionic.
If we thought we had enthusiasm,
Now we are bubbling over
With a zest for life that enthuses others.

Sometimes it is hard to believe that this can be true – yet another great encouragement! I just love that picture of the eagle swooping out of the sky to rescue her baby eaglet as it plummets to the earth in its failed attempt at learning to fly. God is able to swoop down and scoop us up also – he never lets us fall quite the distance.

27

On special offer

We are bombarded by advertisements these days which tell us that we can have something for nothing, that we can buy now and pay later, or pay nothing now. Our common sense tells us that there must be a catch, but how often we are taken in, only to have a rude awakening later when the bills begin to catch up with us and we are in debt.

The gospel is different. Eternal life is free to us. We can have it now and we will not have to pay later. The cost is there, but Jesus has looked after that.

Isaiah was telling everyone this hundreds of years before Jesus came.

Isaiah 55 God says it's all free!

Hey, don't you see?
It's all free!
Life is free
And it's abundant.
But the transaction is the same as if you'd paid the
    going price.

What does that mean?
It means that you don't need the things you think
    you need.

What you need is a different perspective on life.
So be careful how you spend this wonderful,
    abundant life.
It is an abundance you can revel in,
So be mindful where it comes from.
It comes from God,
And we need to listen to God,
Because he is the one with the words of life.
He is the one with whom we make the transaction.
He is the one who makes a covenant with us
And it is much bigger than just ourselves and him,
Much bigger than just us and our friends.

Don't miss the boat!
Don't be too late!
Don't miss the opportunity!
It's *now* that God is waiting for you.
It is *now* that he is near.
So take the opportunity while it is here.
Take the risk.
Come to God
Because God's love for you knows no bounds
And whatever you have done,
However much you may have disbelieved,
He is there waiting
With wide open arms.
He will enfold you in his arms, in his love,
And never let you go.

We think we know all the answers.
We think we can sort things out.
We think we know best –
But we haven't a clue.

Our ways are not heavenly,
They are earthbound
And they are so often wrong.

Just as the rain does its job
And gives life to the earth,
So God's word gives life to us.
And even though we may try not to hear it
Still it will fulfil God's purpose.
It will nourish us and set us on the right path.

Just as it is hard to imagine the mountains and the
    hills singing
Or the trees clapping their hands,
In difficult times it is hard to imagine joy and peace.
But I have seen the grass alive in the wind
And the branches of the trees waving and dipping,
I have heard the music of the birds,
The rustling of the trees
And the singing of the wind.
So God's promise of life abundant
Is true –
In fact it is there for us to collect.

What an amazing message! The certainty and assurance just ring out through this passage. I found myself wondering why we are so slow to understand, so reluctant sometimes to live as though we believe what God is telling us. When we start to doubt, it is an excellent exercise to recall the things that have happened in our lives when we have seen God at work. We need to remind ourselves that God has been involved in our lives in the past, and he is involved now – in which case life is to be lived to the full.

A friend who was going through a particularly difficult time was very excited one evening, as he drove home on a dark and very windy night, when his headlights picked out the cow parsley waving frantically at the side of the road. It reminded him of the verses in this passage which say that the trees of the field will clap their hands. It was as if the cow parsley was praising God, and was a great reminder to him that God is faithful.

28

What is God telling me?

Many of us will be familiar with the following words:

"How lovely on the mountains are the feet of him who brings good news, proclaiming peace, announcing news of happiness" (Isaiah 52:7).

Even if we have not read the passage in Isaiah, we will probably have sung the hymn with the chorus "Our God reigns". I have always thought that the bearer of good news was Jesus – that this was Isaiah foretelling the One to come who would both give good news and be the good news. However, more recently I have come to look at the passage differently.

This is how the New King James Version translates Isaiah:52:7–10:

"How beautiful upon the mountains
Are the feet of him who brings good news,
Who proclaims peace,
Who brings glad tidings of good things,
Who proclaims salvation,
Who says to Zion
"Your God reigns!"
Your watchmen shall lift up their voices,
With their voices they shall sing together;
For they shall see eye to eye

When the Lord brings back Zion.
Break forth into joy, sing together,
You waste places of Jerusalem!
For the Lord has comforted His people,
He has redeemed Jerusalem.
The Lord has made bare His holy arm
In the eyes of all the nations;
And all the ends of the earth shall see
The salvation of our God."

I was reminded of my responsibility to share the Good News of everything that God had done for me when I remembered the passage from Ephesians that we looked at earlier, which talks about having our feet shod with the preparation of the gospel of peace.

Oh dear, how we tremble in our shoes at the thought that we're expected to "share our faith". So much for beautiful feet, which is the language Isaiah uses. I don't know about you but I don't think of my feet as being beautiful – and while I love to bring good news, and get very excited about it, I'm not so good at being enthusiastic about the gospel. Yet the gospel is the *very best news* we could possibly have, and people do actually want to hear it.

It is easy to be scared of talking about the things that matter to us but, if only we make an effort, God *can* use us. If we are really excited about God, how can we keep quiet? People are longing to hear and, if we dare to open our mouths, God will cover for us. We may stumble over our words, but God will sort them out so that the hearers will understand.

As I allowed the familiar words to "come at me", I began to catch something of the excitement of the salvation of God – the good news – and to see how important it was for me to share that good news. What is more, God would help me do it.

Isaiah 52:7–10 Bringing Good News

The bearer of Good News
Will be so pleased with what he has to tell everyone
That he will have a great big grin on his face!
And it will be catching.
A smile will spread across every face.
People will watch his approach with growing excitement.

Those who bring Good News
Will also bring peace,
And, along with the smile,
Have a beautiful tranquillity about them.

How wonderful it is to hear the news:
"It's OK. You are safe.
Everything is all right.
God is in control.
All is well."

The expectant hush
Will be broken
By a murmur of voices
As everyone breathes a sigh of relief.
The murmur will rise to a babble,
The babble will rise
To an excited rumbling of sound.
Everyone will want
To shout and sing to God.

Broken friendships will be restored.
Every view will seem more beautiful.
Everyone will feel comforted,

Feel they belong,
Feel part of a big, loving family.

Everyone
Will see a little more of the beauty
And power of God.
And many will see more of God,
Understand more of his message,
And want to be part of his family,
Dwelling in safety
And comfort
And peace.

God seemed to be saying to me, "Yes, this *is* Jesus Isaiah is foreseeing, but there are some things here for you too. Yes, this was written at a specific time and there is a message in it specific to the people of that time. But there are lots of messages in it and, if you listen carefully, if you open yourself up to the big picture, there is a very special message here for you."

29

"Recognize this Man?"

I don't know what your mental picture of Jesus is, but I like mine to be a comfortable one. I like to think of Jesus as a safe person to be with, someone who is in control, someone who is able to look after me, someone who is personable and charismatic, who draws people to himself, who carries them along in his enthusiasm, who is very wise and always has an answer, a solution, to the problem. I like to think that this is a fairly accurate picture.

But there is another picture which we don't like to think about too much – it is quite thought-provoking and challenging. It is not found in the New Testament, as you might think, but in Isaiah.

Isaiah 53 The One who takes the blame

You are not going to believe this.
It is not what you are expecting.
God is going to send someone to help us.
Be he won't be quite what you imagine is needed.

He won't be born in a palace
And brought up as royalty,
Groomed to lead people,
And be their king.

In fact, no-one will really notice his childhood.
When he grows up he won't be a film star,
A budding footballer,
A handsome lead singer,
Or a great politician.
Everyone will think him very ordinary –
In fact they will not count him important at all.
He will not seem trendy,
Rich,
Be seen in all the right places.
He will be ignored.
Everyone will be much too busy
Pursuing wealth and happiness,
Trying to be important,
To gain fame and recognition,
To notice or be bothered about him.
We won't want to be seen with him.
If we meet him in the street
We will run away and pretend we didn't see him.
He will be so sad and serious –
No-one will have any time for him.
He will be poor,
Sleeping in the streets,
And everyone will think it serves him right.
He will be arrested
And accused of all sorts of dreadful things
And we will think it's his own fault.
We will make all sorts of accusations:
He's brought it on himself;
He probably does drugs;
He's probably a thief;
He's probably killed someone.
Such a shady person,

Always in bad company,
Nothing he did would surprise us!

And all the time it's we who are in trouble.
We should have been the ones arrested.
He may have been around the drug dealers,
The riff-raff,
But all the time he was innocent of any wrongdoing.
He is just taking the blame so we don't get into trouble.
We are all so busy doing our own thing,
Ignoring God,
And meanwhile
This guy takes the blame for everything.

Just by letting these words from Isaiah sink into us we have a very up-to-date picture, as well as one of what happened 2000 years ago. It takes us into the next part of the story, which God also reveals in the Old Testament.

30

No life without hope

You can tell from its title that Lamentations is not the most jolly of books. But in it I found a little nugget of gold which reminded me how important it is to have hope. Not hope as we use the word in modern-day English. When we hope for something to happen, we don't necessarily expect it to. It's a bit like making a wish. But hope in Lamentations meant a sure certainty that something great would happen.

Lamentations 3:21–26 I almost forgot

Whoops! I almost forgot.
I was just so bogged down in my troubles,
Calling them all to mind
And feeling sorry for myself,
That I forgot about hope.
I forgot about God.
I forgot that he loves me.
As long as he loves me it will be all right.
After all, everything comes to an end eventually
Except for God's mercies.
They don't just last for ever
They renew themselves every day.
As surely as the sun rises every morning,
God is always there.

And he will still be there when the sun stops rising.
He is my "main man".
He is the one I will seek after.
I may have to wait,
And wait,
But the wait will be worth it.
I need to wait without all this complaining
Because God will come up trumps in the end.

It is said that if we don't have hope we have no reason to live, and we die. Jesus certainly gives us hope – hope for each day and hope for eternity.

31

All this and heaven, too?

I often hear people say that they are looking forward to heaven. I am surprised about that. I find it difficult to agree with it, or even to believe that they are being honest. After all, life here on earth is great. There are lots of things I still want to do. There are many things to enjoy. And I don't really know what heaven will be like. I'm glad that I have the certain hope of being there one day – but not just yet.

Perhaps that's why I found and enjoyed this short chapter in Isaiah. Such a lovely description must surely be of heaven. I think that maybe God was saying something to me.

Isaiah 35 A world of glory

Just imagine –
Lush vegetation in every shade of green;
Huge and beautiful flowers in every colour and hue;
Warm sunshine and soft refreshing rain;
Beauty and grandeur all around;
Birds singing such lovely songs,
You never want them to stop;
The sky alight and glowing with the glory of God.

How shall we survive long enough to see all this?
Only if you help us as we hobble along.

Only if you encourage us to carry on.
For we are full of fear and weariness.
Help us to hang in there,
So that we can enjoy the wonders you will bring to pass.

What must it be like to live in a world of darkness,
Never seeing anyone or anything?
Relying on other people's descriptions,
Which are so inadequate.
What will it be like to be able to see?
Will the world seem very big and bright?

What must it be like to live in a world of silence,
Never knowing when someone is approaching?
Not hearing their footfall,
Never hearing laughter – or tears.
Never hearing the sound of the sea
Or the wind or thunder.
And then suddenly there is sound
So loud that it hurts.
What will it feel like if, one minute, every step you take
Is painful and slow,
And the next is a giant leap up the side of a mountain as
    if you had wings?
What will it be like for those who have never uttered
    a word
And always found it difficult to communicate?
They won't be able to stop talking!
Where there was nothing,
There will be everything beyond our wildest imagination.

And then we shall see the way to go,
The safe path upward.

Will we dare to take that route
When we read the name –
"Highway of holiness"?
Is that the way for us?
Once on it we'll not be able to get off.
It will be safe.
We will be so glad, we will sing and make merry
And forget all our sorrows.
But we need to get on it.

These verses are a little reminder that the world we live in is fallen, imperfect, but the world we are going to is perfect in every way.

32

God's treasure house

God has so many great things in store for us, in this world –
wonderful things to be discovered all around us, in our friendships, in our everyday lives, and in God's word. We need to be
open to them. As I've tried to be open to God's word, I have
made lots of great discoveries.

God wants the very best for us, and will respond as we open
ourselves to him. This one little verse in Isaiah says a lot, if you
read behind it:

Isaiah 30:18 Wonderful things in store

God has a store
Of the most wonderful things
Which are intended just for you.
And he will wait as long as it takes
For the right moment
To give them to you –
The moment when you are ready to receive them.
How great will be your love for him then.
You will worship and adore him
And marvel
That his mercy is so enormous
And his justice, too.
It is hard to understand

How this can be.
If only we would wait for God
In the same manner
As he waits for us,
We would come to know
The rich meaning
Of the word *blessed*.

I have certainly been richly blessed as I have allowed God's word to "come at me", and I am sure that you can experience the same blessing from God too. So – in the last section of this book I shall dare to make a few suggestions, hoping that you will dare to let God's word "come at you" in a new way and discover more of the great store-house of treasure that God is keeping for you.

PART FOUR

Over to You

33

God's amazing word

Sometimes I think I have a bee in my bonnet about the Bible. I so long for people to read it, to be excited about it. It seems that so often we either take it for granted, or we ignore it. Are you, like me, a great prevaricator? I always want to put off until tomorrow what I know I should do today. But we don't really know what tomorrow will bring, and we need to do today the things that are important. Yes, God's word has always been there, and it always will be, but that doesn't mean that we don't need to do anything about it. It is important – we ignore it at our peril. It is our instruction manual and, if we don't follow God's instructions, life doesn't work very well,

Psalm 119:89–112 "I do love your word"

Your word has always been fixed in heaven
From the very beginning.
It is well established and can never be moved.
So your plan has been in place from the very beginning
And you have stuck by it through the ages.

What you started you will finish.
You set the earth in place and it will stand firm.
It will always run according to your rules –
For you designed it.

You gave your marching orders for the way things work.
You call the tune.
So if I ignore your way how can I survive?
Nothing will work properly.
I need to take pleasure in the way you have
    organised things.
So I can never really forget your word.
I may push it away from me sometimes,
I may even choose to ignore it –
But I can never forget it.
For it has given me a meaning to life
Without which I would not survive.

I do belong to you, really –
Please keep me when I wander away.
Remind me of your word and its power.
It's often so tempting to be lazy,
Not to bother,
To put other things first,
To want to do my own things,
To have time for myself –
But I have only to read your word
To realise that I am missing so much
That you want me to have.

I have had glimpses of your glory;
I know it's real.
I know I want it to be reflected in me.

How amazingly wide and all-embracing your word is.
You never want to miss anyone out –
You always want there to be room.
I do love your word, really –

I just let other things push it out.
How silly I am.

There is so much of your word;
I could meditate on it for ever –
All day and every day –
And there is always something more.
It is always there.

By reading your word I can be wise.
I can be stronger in my resolve not to be distracted from
     your word –
For there are always distractions.
I sometimes feel unhappy when I hear what others say.
Somehow it doesn't seem quite right,
Yet who am I to question?
I read your word and I try to see what it is saying to me.
Maybe it says something else to others.
But it's hard to stick to my beliefs
When those who are older and wiser seem to say
     something different.
I must just keep asking:
"What is your word saying to *me*?"

Every so often I remember your word,
And pull back from the path I am treading.
I have not really left your teachings,
But every so often I wander.

How lovely it is to read your word
And let it speak to me.
It always has something new to say
And it is such a comfort.

Sometimes I read with new insight.
I wonder why I didn't see that before
And why I am so silly as to let you down.

How I need understanding,
An insight into what I should be doing.
Your word *does* have answers –
If I spend time looking.
It *does* make things clear.
It *does* tell me which way to go.
If I spend time with you, suddenly the light dawns.
How often have I resolved to try harder,
To listen,
To read your word,
To do what it says.

But it is so hard –
I let you down so often.
I give up when the going gets tough.

You have the power to change me, Lord,
To enter my life and charge it with power,
To rekindle my love and resolve every time it nearly
    fades away.
Your word promises me that you will do this.
I find it hard to make promises
In case I don't keep them.
But I *do* love you, Lord –
Please take my love and increase it.
And teach me what your love really means.
I so often try to live my life
My way
For *me* –

But somehow your word always comes back to me.
Distractions are all around me –
I am so often ready to give up –
But you always bring me back to your word.
Your word –
Which you have given me as an inheritance –
Is mine.
It warms my heart –
Seeping into me like the sunshine,
Giving me a sense of well-being and peace.
I so want to follow you – always.

Is this psalm the story of your life? It certainly is of mine. As these words came into my mind, I found them reflecting back to me the way I felt, the way life was for me, and particularly how my reading of God's word affected my life, even when I didn't realise it. It encourages me to press on with discovering and owning God's word for myself, and in so doing discovering and owning God for myself.

So I invite you to put *yourself* in front of God's word. Let it speak to you. Expect it to identify with you. Expect it to have something very special to say to you.

34

Crashing waves and the incoming tide

I have found it difficult to describe the "writings" I have shared in this book.

I have not paraphrased the passages.

I have not studied the passages in great depth and read lots of background material.

Although I have often thought of it as "re-writing" the passages, that is not what I'm doing. None of us has permission to re-write the Bible.

A little illustration may help me explain what I think has taken place.

I used to live in Gloucestershire, about as far from the sea as you can get. Every year we went on a Sunday school outing to the seaside. And I longed, one day, to live beside the sea, where the waves would crash onto the beach, and the sea would come at me. Well, I do live by the sea now, though it's not quite what I had in mind then. I think God showed his sense of humour in bringing me to Tollesbury, which is on an estuary where the tide creeps slowly in to cover the saltmarsh before slowly creeping out again.

I find these two pictures – of the tide creeping in and out, and waves crashing onto the beach – a useful way of explaining what happens when I find myself writing down what I read in the Bible in different words.

As I have spent time with God's word, opening my mind to

it, a particular passage addresses itself to me more and more directly. As I have let God's word come at me, much as the waves of the sea come at us on the beach on a wild and windy day, I have been able to express what God seems to be saying to me in new words. They have seeped into my being in the same way that the sea creeps up the estuary as the tide comes in. And just as the sea deposits a new layer of silt on the saltings, so it is as if God has deposited some of his truth in a new way upon my heart. I have to make sure that these new insights don't just seep away again with the turn of the tide – which is why I have taken to writing them down.

Here is Psalm 8 as an example. I've placed my words after the Bible verses they reflect on. I generally use the New King James Version, as here, because I love the language – but the version does not matter.

> *O LORD, our Lord,*
> *How excellent is Your name in all the earth,*
> *You have set your glory*
> *above the heavens!*

What a very excellent God you are.

> *Out of the mouth of babes and infants*
> *You have ordained strength,*
> *Because of your enemies,*
> *That you may silence the enemy and the avenger.*
> *When I consider your heavens,*
> *the work of your fingers,*
> *The moon and the stars,*
> *which you have ordained,*

I think I understood it better when I was a child.
I had no trouble then

Believing that you made the world
Just like that.
The moon and the stars
And all that space up there,
The hills and the valleys,
The mountains and the rivers.
Wow! The first time that I saw mountains -
Awesome!
I think I felt OK in the midst of it all.
Now?
Well, I feel how very little I am in the scheme of things.
Small and insignificant,
Unimportant.

What is man that you are mindful of him,
*   And the son of man that you visit him?*
For you have made him a little lower than the angels,
*   And you have crowned him with glory and honour.*

But your view is a bit different, it seems.
You have made me very important.
You honour me,
When I should be the one giving honour to you.
You surround me with your glory,
Your very specialness.
Somehow it seems the wrong way round.

You have made him to have dominion over the works of your hands;
*   You have put all things under his feet,*
All sheep and oxen –
*   Even the beasts of the field,*
The birds of the air,
*   And the fish of the sea*
*   That pass through the paths of the seas.*

What is more, you have given me things to do in this
    world of yours.
For it is your world, not mine.
And you've set my feet upon this earth
And allowed me to walk upon it.
You've even put down the path for me.

> *O LORD, our Lord,*
>   *How excellent is Your name in all the earth!*

You are a very excellent God.
Why do you bother with little old me?
Is it because the path is important,

I am important,
And it is important that I keep my feet on the path?

You are so very excellent
I really should do that, shouldn't I?

You will notice that some things are missed out, other things
expanded on, as I have set my mind free to meditate on a
particular verse, or a few verses together. Coming back to a
passage later, and working out where my writing fits in, helps
me to see how I may have "read behind the lines", or just let
my thoughts range a bit more widely.

Maybe you could take this psalm and ask yourself, what is
it saying to you? Somehow, trying to capture a thought in
different words, or letting a particular word catch our imagination, gives us a starting-point. It can set us free to reflect on
the rest of the psalm or passage and make it our own.

If you want to open yourself to God in this way, find a psalm that is special to you, or a verse in a psalm that means something special to you. Spend time reading the whole psalm over to yourself. Think about what is being said, who is saying it to whom, and then try to discover how it is speaking to you, and own it for yourself.

35

Get ready for some fun!

Sometimes, by letting a word catch your imagination, you can come up with a fun thought which may sound a bit crazy, and yet you have grasped a nugget of truth which can be a good starting-point. If you are open to this, it can lead to further surprises.

I was once using Bible reading notes which directed me to 1 Thessalonians chapter 4. Verse 1 in my version talked about "abounding" more and more and, in the same verse, "walking" to please God. The writer of the notes had headed the page "Bounding along with God". This really captured my imagination. I had this wonderful picture of bounding along the road, skipping and dancing, jumping for joy, going at a great speed, full of fun and enjoyment. This is how that thought led me on, as I read the verses that followed:

1 Thessalonians 4:1–8 Bounding along with God

Don't just walk with God,
Bound along with him.
You know what you should be doing to please God,
So do it in style.
God just longs for you to get it right
And to be right alongside him.
Don't spoil things.

Keep yourselves clean and pure
Or God will be ashamed to be seen with you.
If you are to honour God,
You need to honour yourself,
Body, mind and soul.
Don't listen to those who say
"It's OK to forget God for a while.
You can't possibly live up to his standards,
So let yourself go."
God is there with you –
He knows your thoughts and actions
And he cannot sanction anything
Which falls short of purity and goodness.
God has called us to be like him,
To be worthy of bounding along by his side.
If we think he doesn't notice our wrongdoings
We are mistaken.
If we don't want to walk with him for a while,
We're really saying we don't want to walk with him at all.
He doesn't want our half-hearted presence.
He wants us to bound along with him.

It was a strange kind of analogy – the passage wasn't really about those first enthusiastic thoughts I'd had – but that phrase, "bounding along with God", threw a really new light on what God expected of me. No half-hearted measures, no creeping around, no being content with less than the best, no giving God just the few bits I wanted to part with, no going half the distance.

I still laugh when I read that passage, and it helps me to remember that God asks for our whole being. Over the top!

36

What is God saying – to me and to you?

I'm very conscious that what I have been sharing with you is really all about how God's word has "come at *me*", how it has spoken to me, how it has changed the way I read the Bible, how it excites me and teaches me. I have simply had a heart response to God's word.

I am not a scholar or an expert. I don't know the original Hebrew or Greek. I haven't written a translation or a paraphrase. It is simply what the passage is saying to me, about me and about God.

I would like to think that my offerings will in some way give you permission to reflect on the Bible using your own words to make it personally relevant to you and to help you identify with what God wants to say to you.

I am more than ever convinced that if we are able to read God's word in an open way, expecting it to speak to us, and willing to make an effort when the going gets tough, it will have an effect upon us. For there's no pretence in God's word. Life is how it is. Life is real. These words are relevant to us; they identify with us.

More than that, they supply the missing link between God and each one of us, and how we live our lives. Without this personal communication we have only glimpses of God and his purpose for us.

I am still amazed when I find a new piece of scripture that

"comes at me" afresh, in different words. And I don't have a monopoly on the process. You too can know the excitement of discovering God's word and owning it for *yourself*. Why not try?

Turn back to any of the passages we have looked at, find it in your own Bible, and discover what it has to say about you and about God. Best of all, find a completely new passage of the Bible and "let it come at you" afresh. It may not happen straight away – be patient and prepare for a surprise.

We are all very precious to God and he wants us to discover new things from his word every day. It was my meditation on Mary's song in Luke 1:46–55 that made me realise how very precious *I* was to God. At first it felt presumptuous to express this passage in my own words. I am very conscious that they don't encapsulate all that Mary is saying – but here they are. As you read this passage for yourselves, see what else it says.

Luke 1:46–55 Mary's Song

Isn't the Lord just great?
My whole being wants to run and sing
And tell the whole world
How wonderful God is.
I am only a young girl,
Nothing special.
Yet everyone for all time
Is going to think I'm *very* special
Because God has made me so.

What is more,
Because he has made me special
He will be able to make everyone special –
For ever.
People won't understand

Because God turns everything upside-down.
The things we think are special
Are not special at all.
The people we think are important
Are not important at all.
He remembers and honours those who honour him.
He keeps his promises to them.

37

Over to you

Sometimes we think that we know all there is to know about a passage – we may not be very good at obeying what it says, taking the instructions on board, but we think it is fairly straightforward. I think this is one of the reasons why I stayed away from passages in the New Testament at first. It was somehow easier to have a heart response to a psalm than to one of Paul's exhortations.

But there's no need to be afraid of a very familiar passage. It can be a good place to begin. Maybe you already have a favourite that you could think yourself into in a slightly different way. All you have to do is be open, spend time with God's word, be ready to listen – and have a pen and paper handy.

Why not take 1 Corinthians 13, that great chapter on love? I began one day on verses 4–8. I asked myself how much I loved, what love really meant, what was the mechanism of love?

I hit on the phrase "If my heart is really filled up with God's love" as a beginning for each of the five verses and then set my mind free on the rest of the words.

You might use my phrase, or come up with one of your own, and then write in your own words what these verses are describing. Ask yourself questions – what does being kind really mean? What does it entail? How do you show kindness? See what you come up with: you may surprise yourself.

My questions and reflection so excited me that, eventually, I wrote out the whole chapter in different words which challenged me to think what it was really about. I also found that it was easy to separate the verses out. It helped me realise it was about much more than love. And it may help you, too.

Before you read my reflections – work on your own. It will be worth the effort.

1 Corinthians 13 Filled up with God's love

[1]Even if I have the most eloquent speech, a real way with words, and even if people are drawn to listen to me, if I don't love you, Lord, and if I don't love the people I am talking to, I'm really just enjoying the sound of my own voice.

[2]Even if I have worked out some of the answers, even if I have real insight about what is going to happen, even if I believe with my whole heart, if I don't really love you, if my heart is not filled with love, it is empty and I am of no significance to you or anyone.

[3]If I am very generous to those around me – even if I give everything away, even if I am always doing things for people, even if I always put other's needs before my own – if it is not love that stirs and prompts me, if it's just that I want to be noticed or loved or to receive some kind of reward, there's no point; there will be no blessing for me or anyone else as a result of my action.

[4]If my heart is really filled up with God's love, I will always have time for people, nothing will be too much trouble. I will be kind and caring, longing to make other people's lives richer by acts of kindness and help.

If my heart is really filled up with God's love, I shall not be jealous of the things that other people have. I shall not feel sorry for myself and think I am hard done by, neither shall I be thinking of myself all the time, ignoring other people and treating them as unimportant.

⁵I shall not be rude and pushy, making sure I get what I want at the expense of others.

If my heart is really filled up with God's love, no matter what happens, what people say, I shall know God's peace and contentment in my soul. I shall not get all stirred up and resentful. I shall not retaliate with words and deeds. I shall not keep a scoresheet of other people's wrongdoings.

⁶If my heart is really filled up with God's love, I shall not be interested in gossip, in gloating over other people's failures, in spreading rumours, in recounting the misfortunes of others. I shall want to talk about the things that matter, the truths of God's word and his love, the great things he has done for us, the things he has taught us. I shall want to praise God and tell everyone how great he is.

⁷If my heart is really filled up with God's love, I shall be a tower of strength when others need help. I shall be an encourager of others. I shall have a strong and sure faith, believing totally in the word of God and its power to help and work in our lives, and I shall be sure that one day Jesus will come again and give me my inheritance. He will never, ever let me down. I will be able to survive whatever circumstances come my way and I shall never give up, whatever happens to me.

⁸If my heart is really filled up with God's love, that is better than an insurance policy. It is fail safe. Nothing can destroy it or make it stop working.

⁹Things that we experience and are familiar with, things that we come to rely on in this world, are not really reliable at all. Even things which come from God – gifts from God that help and encourage us in our Christian lives – ¹⁰will not continue for ever. They won't be needed to prop us up any more when Jesus comes again.

[11]We sometimes think we know all the answers, that we have arrived, that we have been spiritually blessed in tremendous ways, but we don't know the half of what God has in store for us.

[12]When we really arrive it will blow our minds, and we will realise that we know nothing. For we see and know only a very pale reflection of what God has in store for us. When we see him face to face, everything will be the right way round. We shall see him as he really is, and all he has been saving for us.

[13]For the moment we have to rely upon our faith, our hope and our love, all of which God has given to us to enable us to travel our journey. Our faith and our hope may waiver and change, but let us make sure that our love remains steadfast. For God's love in us is the power for our lives; it makes our lives effective and meaningful and means that we live as God intended. It means we're running on the right fuel and we'll get to the end of our journey safely.

You may think that your meditations are just for you, or you may find opportunity to share them. I have used my meditations in articles, and to back-up talks and illustrations. I have also used them as a basis for prayers. Sometimes that's been just for me and at other times I have found them helpful when I've been asked to lead the prayers at church.

Just how you can share your own meditations – your personal discoveries from God's amazing word as you make it your own – is something I can leave you to think about. For me, it's been the most wonderful discovery that has transformed my life with God and the people around me. I hope you learn to enjoy owning God's word for yourself. Over to you!

"When I get to heaven"

We think life on earth is very important, and we live as if it will last for ever, but of course it won't. None of us knows how long our life on earth will last. But we can know that our life with God will last for ever. As I said earlier on, it's hard to think of heaven as where we want to be right now. Our feet are so firmly planted on the ground that it is difficult to imagine another kind of life. However much we read the Bible or say our prayers, I am sure heaven will be full of surprises for all of us.

For me, Psalm 84 is about arriving in heaven, although being in "God's house" is often thought of as being in church (in the Psalmist's day, God's Temple in Jerusalem). As I have said, when life is good here on earth, I don't think we really long to be in heaven. Yet the more I read about heaven in the Bible, particularly when I read a Psalm like this one, I think, "Hey it'll be good to be there – but not yet."

I wanted to include this Psalm here because, even though I had written it out, I didn't really understand what it was saying until an experience I had later filled it with meaning. So if you feel any passage speaking to you, although you can't really identify with what it's saying at the moment, tuck it away in a safe place. You will certainly want to return to it later.

Psalm 84 At home in God's "mansion"

It must be so wonderful in your house, Lord!
How I long to see it.
It will be so lovely
To be there with you.
I guess everyone has a place where they feel really
    at home.
Even the common sparrow has a place he goes back to.
Even the swallow, who travels a lot,
Likes to make a nest and settle in.
We love to have somewhere we truly belong.

How wonderful to be in your house with you;
To really belong there.
I bet those who are there can't stop saying *"Thankyou!"*

If I really relied upon your strength for the journey,
What a journey that would be!
Through every kind of terrain,
Every kind of climate,
And then to arrive –
Safe at last.
How wonderful
That you have provided us with help:
Jesus,
Who shields us
And presents us at the gates of your mansion
Where you will look at us and say
"Welcome!"

I think I'd rather have the chance of just a peep,
Or even to stand outside the door,

Than never come near.
Will I really be able see you?
Will I really not be with the wicked?
Your warmth and light draw me to you.
I know I'll be safe there with you.
And if I walk with Jesus,
You will give me every good thing.
You are just longing for me
To receive everything you have in store for me.
Nothing will be kept back.

What a reward there is for the person who trusts in you.
A safe place,
A home with you, Lord.

It seems that we will have a great welcome. I knew this in my head, but it wasn't until I had a rather interesting experience that I knew it in my heart.

I once went on a pilgrimage where there were about 3000 people, all seeming very sure of themselves and what it was all about. I was late. Everyone was already gathering for the open-air service, so I thought I would just pop into the little stone chapel, which was the focus of the pilgrimage – it would be empty now, so I'd have an opportunity to be there on my own. I made my way to the chapel and went up to the door. As I reached out to push the door, it opened before I could touch it.

When the man standing there saw me, recognition flitted across his face, and then he looked totally non-plussed. I smiled and said "Hello", but he put up his hand as though to push me back – a defensive, "you-can't-come-in" gesture. Then I realised that he had a bevy of bishops (and a cardinal!) behind him and that they were starting their procession to the big stage from which they were going to lead the service.

I retreated quickly, feeling really stupid and in the way. Why hadn't someone told me? Then I realised that everyone was standing round waiting with cameras – and I felt even worse. Of course, I was careful not to show it, but my mind was racing as I tried not to be self-conscious, though I felt as if everyone was looking at me. It was really dreadful.

When their little posse had moved off, I went into the chapel with a few other people. I tried to collect my thoughts, but I was so disconcerted that I didn't quite know what to do. Telling myself it didn't matter, that it was good to be there, and telling God I'm not quite sure what, I made my way out into the sunshine and looked to see where I should go for the service. I wandered through the masses of people sitting and standing around and found an empty spot just as the "important" people made their way to the stage.

As I watched all the folk up on the stage – especially all those important bishops – I was still thinking about my feelings at the chapel door. And I began to wonder if it would be like that when I got to heaven. I had been quite excited to arrive at the chapel, and being "pushed out" had actually upset me. I imagined arriving in heaven, really excited to be there, longing to enter in, to see Jesus at last. What if there was an angel saying, "Sorry, you can't come in here. God is far too important for you to come near." And I began to cry. The tears rolled down my face as I considered what it would mean if I was rejected and pushed away when I got to heaven.

Then I realised that it would not be like that. Jesus would be at the door himself, with his arms open wide. And he would be saying, "Welcome! Come in. We've been waiting for you especially. It's so good to see you." *It would be OK.* Just as it is lovely to arrive home after a long journey and be where everything is safe and familiar, so it will be in heaven; and at last we will be able to rest and feel that we truly belong.

Then I began to think about all those important people again. I'm not much into pomp and circumstance, and people being important. They make me feel clumsy and small. But I understood that everything had to be organised and that all those bishops needed to be looked after, and the more I thought about it the more I realised that in the same situation I would not have known what to do myself. It occurred to me that if we feel trapped or uncertain what to do next, if we feel threatened by a situation, it's easy to react in the wrong way. It's easy to put up barriers and push people away until we feel safe again. And how does that make *them* feel? Sometimes we push people away when we are busy or anxious; we don't give them time; we make them feel in the way. Well, it's a good thing that God doesn't do that. He is the most important person ever, but he would never push us away, or make us feel like that. There's no chance that we will only be allowed to peep in at the door. We'll be dragged inside and given a place of honour.

The strange thing was, I didn't fully own this experience or understand it until I remembered this Psalm. It is an experience I will never forget. In fact it is two experiences: the event, which makes for a fun story, and the feeling that was so real it became reinforced by the Psalm. Now it is so embedded in my very being that I could never doubt my welcome in heaven. The Bible is able to do this for us – the experience would not have been the same without the Psalm.